QUMRAN

To
Father Roland de Vaux
remembered with respect and great affection

CITIES OF THE BIBLICAL WORLD

Qumran

Philip R. Davies

Lecturer in Biblical Studies,
University of Sheffield

LUTTERWORTH PRESS
GUILDFORD, SURREY

General Editor:
Graham I. Davies, Lecturer in Divinity, Cambridge University.

Other Titles:
Excavation in Palestine, Roger Moorey, Senior Assistant Keeper,
    Department of Antiquities, Ashmolean Museum, Oxford.
Jericho, John R. Bartlett, Lecturer in Divinity and Fellow of
    Trinity College, Dublin.

In Preparation:
Beersheba and Arad, Graham I. Davies.
Ugarit (Ras Shamra), Adrian H. W. Curtis, Lecturer in Old
    Testament Studies, University of Manchester.

First published in 1982
Copyright © Philip R. Davies 1982

ISBN 0–7188–2458–X

Set in 10/12pt. Plantin

Printed and bound in Great Britain at
The Camelot Press Ltd, Southampton

Contents

List of Illustrations

Note: The maps and plans should not be taken as infallibly accurate in every
case. While care has been taken to render them both clear and correct, they
are designed only for consultation in connection with the text of this book.
For detailed information and for clarification, it is advisable to consult
official ordnance maps of the West Bank and the information contained in
the reports of the excavations published in the *Revue Biblique*.

Preface

Until the discovery of the Dead Sea Scrolls in 1947 and the subsequent excavation of Khirbet Qumran, the existence of a Jewish settlement near the Dead Sea remained unsuspected by biblical scholars. Apart from one possible allusion in the Old Testament, the site is unrecorded in the Bible and certainly no hint emerges from its pages of the fascinating community which inhabited it in Jesus' own day.

Yet the Scrolls have revolutionised our perception of Judaism in the time of Jesus. They have provided us with the only substantial corpus of Jewish literature from his age and revealed ideas and customs which force us to reassess the relationship between Jesus' ministry and that of the early church with its Jewish enviroment. Thanks to the discovery of Qumran, we can appreciate the richness and variety of beliefs, speculations, hopes and rituals which characterised Judaism in the first century AD. Dare I say that as a result biblical scholars have been forced to redefine their understanding of this Judaism, and abandon that facile opposition of Christianity and Judaism to which many have been prone. If Qumran is not itself part of our biblical heritage, its witness has immeasurably enriched our own appreciation of that heritage. Indeed, much of the literature of the Qumran community would not have disgraced the pages of our Christian scriptures.

I owe thanks to the following for their help in preparing this book: Jerry Murphy-O'Connor of the École Biblique for sparing time and trouble despite the call of more pressing obligations; my colleague, David Hill, for suggested improvements of both style and substance; Malcolm Reeve and Robert Marshall for proof-reading and proving a sample of 'audience reaction'; Miss Sheila Ottewell of the Sheffield University Department of Geography for providing fine maps and plans from my own poor originals; Graham Davies, the editor of the series and the staff of Lutterworth Press for advice, assistance – and patience; and my wife, Carol, my partner in everything.

Abbreviations

A.D.D.S.   R. de Vaux, *Archaeology and the Dead Sea Scrolls*, Oxford University Press, 1972.

B.A.S.O.R. *Bulletin of the American Schools of Oriental Research*, New Haven.

D.S.S.E.   G. Vermes, *The Dead Sea Scrolls in English*, second edition, Penguin, 1975.

D.S.S.   G. Vermes, *The Dead Sea Scrolls. Qumran in Perspective*, Collins, 1977.

An explanation of the system of abbreviations for the Qumran scrolls can be found on page 28.

Acknowledgement

Quotations from *The Dead Sea Scrolls*, tran. Geza Vermesh (second ed. Penguin, 1975) © G. Vermes, 1962, 1965, 1968, 1975 reprinted by permission of Penguin Books Ltd.

Chronological Table

Jewish History	*Qumran Periods*	*Qumran History*
781–740 Uzziah, king of Judah, 'built towers in the wilderness and hewed out many cisterns' (2 Chron. 26:10).	Israelite ↓	Enclosure, rooms, cistern and boundary wall built – at the same time as similar installations on the Buqei'a?
175–164 Antiochus IV (Epiphanes); he sold the High Priesthood, made Jerusalem a Greek *polis*, desecrated the temple and proscribed Judaism.		The 'age of wrath' in which a 'shoot' emerges to 'inherit the Land'.
167 Outbreak of Jewish revolt led by the family of Mattathias (Maccabees).		
164 Judas Maccabaeus restores the Jewish cult to the temple; proscription decree is revoked.		Twenty years of 'groping for the way' by the early Essenes.
160–142 Jonathan, successor to his brother Judas; he assumed the office of High Priest in 152.	Period Ia ↓	*c.* 150–142 (?) The 'Teacher of Righteousness' sets up at Qumran a community, opposed from within the parent movement.

143–134 Simon,
brother of Jonathan,
High Priest and
Ethnarch of the Jews.

134–104 John
Hyrcanus I; quarrels
with Pharisees.
104–103 Aristobulus I;
apparently the first
Hasmonean ruler to
assume the title 'king'.

103–76 Alexander   Period Ib   c. 100 Qumran is
Jannaeus.   ↓   enlarged; many new
                                               members join the
                                               community.

76–67 Alexandra,
Alexander's widow,
reigns; Hyrcanus II is
High Priest.

67–63 Aristobulus,
brother of Hyrcanus II,
usurps kingship.

63 Struggle between
Hyrcanus II and
Aristobulus II; Roman
general Pompey
intervenes and enters
Jerusalem.

63–40 Hyrcanus II
appointed High Priest
only at first; Ethnarch
later.

40–37 Antigonus High
Priest and king;
Parthian invasion 40–38.
Both are opposed by
Herod and the Romans.

37–4 Herod, with Roman support, reigns. Commences rebuilding the temple.		*c.* 31 Qumran is destroyed by fire, caused by military action or earthquake which occurred in 31.
4BC–AD6 Archelaus made Ethnarch of Judaea and Samaria only.	Period II ↓	Essenes return to Qumran and rebuild.
6–41 Judaea ruled by Roman prefects/ procurators.		
41–44 Herod Agrippa I king (cf. Acts 12).		
44–66 Judaea again ruled by Roman procurators; from 50 onwards Agrippa II was king of areas to north and east.		
67–74 Jewish war against Romans; Jerusalem captured in 70, Masada in (probably) 74.	Period III ↓	Qumran captured by Roman soldiers in 68. Until shortly after 74 (?) used as a Roman fort.
132–135 Second Jewish war against Romans, led by Bar Kochba/Kosiba.		Some Jewish fighters briefly occupy Qumran as fort or shelter.

1

The Setting

The ruins of Qumran are situated a mile from the western shore of the Dead Sea, and about three miles from its northern end. The modern city of Jericho and the ruins of two ancient Jerichos are nine miles to the north: Jerusalem lies thirteen miles to the west.

This information will locate the site on a map, but nothing short of a visit will convey the real character of its extraordinary setting. The visitor from Jerusalem, the usual point of departure, will drop from a dry atmosphere at an altitude of 2,400 feet above sea level to an intensely hot and humid basin 1,300 feet below sea level, by means of a modern road which dips and curves between a landscape of dry brown hills. This is the Judaean wilderness, which stretches from the mountains of Judaea to the cliffs overlooking the Dead Sea. The ancient road descended into the Jordan valley along the southern edge of the steep and barren Wadi Qelt, which brings the parable of the Good Samaritan so vividly to mind, and from where it emerged near Jericho a walk of about eight miles in a southerly direction brought the traveller to Qumran. Nowadays the modern road swings south from the Wadi Qelt and forks just north of Nebi Musa; north-east to Jericho and across the Jordan via the Allenby bridge, south-east to the edge of the Dead Sea and thence down the western shore (see map p. 19).

The Dead Sea is not really a sea, but a large and salty lake which is fed by the Jordan, a few small springs and by the seasonal watercourses (wadi in Arabic, nahal in Hebrew). Its waters have no outlet except by evaporation, which accounts for the haze over its surface and the strong tang of the air near its shores. It is famous, of course, for its buoyancy; because of its 30% salt content, it is possible for even a non-swimmer to sit in the water and – a popular tourist pose – read a newspaper. To Arabs and Jews it has been known as the 'Sea of Salt', while the Romans called it 'Lake Asphalt' because of the bitumen which floated in lumps on its surface and could be towed ashore. The name 'Dead Sea' is as apt as either of these. Its waters contain no life[1], its salt and minerals have rendered barren nearly all the shoreline, and, without tide or waves and curiously still most of the time, it gives a distinct impression of lifelessness.

Plate 1   A view of the Qumran outcrop from a cave in the cliffs,
           looking east. The course of the aqueduct can be seen running
           across the neck joining the outcrop to the main terrace. To the
           right of the aqueduct the line of the ancient track can also be
           discerned.

By the shore of the Dead Sea one is standing in the lowest region on the
earth's surface, in a huge rift which stretches right into Africa. On both
sides, the mountains rise steeply almost to sea level, but on the western
shore a beach, or coastal strip, separates the cliffs from the sea. Although a
modern Israeli road now follows this route, in biblical times the main
north-south road, the King's Highway, ran well to the east of the Dead Sea.
Jericho and En-gedi were connected with the other main north-south route
(through Jerusalem and along the ridge of the Judaean highlands) but, as
far as regular traffic went, Qumran lay quite definitely 'off the beaten track'.

At several points this narrow, western coastal strip is interrupted where
the cliffs jut out into the sea, and the most northerly of these points is Ras
Feshkha. But from here northwards the strip gradually widens until at the

northern end of the Dead Sea it is three miles wide. Halfway between Ras Feshkha and this northern end lies Qumran, perched above the coastal plain on an outcrop of the limestone terrace extending along the foot of the cliffs (Plate 1). This outcrop stands 150 feet above the plain and is cut off from the terrace by deep ravines to the south, north and west, except for a narrow neck to the northwest. The main access from the plain is from the northeast, and it is to this corner of the outcrop that a spur of the modern road brings the visitor. From here can be seen almost the entire northern half of the Dead Sea and the coastal road as far south as Ras Feshkha – a good place, one might think, for an observation post or even a military station; for, in addition to its excellent prospect, it occupies a very easily defended position. And this is exactly how Qumran's relatively brief history of occupation ended – and perhaps also began.

But could anyone live at such a place? Looking south from the ruins, one can see less than two miles away down the coastal plain a wide patch of green where the ground is watered by several fresh springs, the main one being ᶜAin Feshkha, which has created an oasis of trees and rushes, a spot which has now become a fairly popular bathing place. It has long been used for watering flocks and herds, and the area is also capable of limited agricultural exploitation. Closer to Qumran, immediately to the south of the outcrop, is the Wadi Qumran, filled once or twice every rainy season by a brief torrent of water cascading from the mountains down to the Dead Sea. Among these mountains, a few miles beyond the cliffs behind Qumran lies a shallow valley called the Buqeiᶜa, which is reached from Qumran by a path leading through the Wadi Qumran. Here, within an hour or two's journey from Qumran, not only can flocks and herds be kept, but cereal crops grown.

The setting of Qumran, then, is not as unfriendly as a first acquaintance with its location suggests. But we have to think of Qumran as only the centre of a wider complex, which comprises the area between the settlement on the outcrop, ᶜAin Feshkha and the Buqeiᶜa beyond the cliffs. In this respect, Qumran is not unlike any other ancient city-state, dependent for the raw materials of life on its surrounding area. However, the resemblance to other cities, as will soon become obvious, goes no further. As a 'biblical city' Qumran is quite unique.

In considering the environment of Qumran, the religious dimension must not be ignored. For those who chose to come and live here during the greater and certainly the most important part of its occupation, between c.150 BC – AD 68, came for religious motives, and the geographical setting of Qumran was regarded by them as symbolic of their predicament. Life in this remote setting was chosen as a deliberate exile, both a physical and spiritual retreat from the mainstream of Jewish life. Almost directly opposite Qumran on the eastern side of the Dead Sea, is the traditional site of Mount Nebo, where Moses had surveyed the Promised Land. For forty years the Israelites had wandered, or more correctly, according to the book of Numbers, marched in military formations of thousands, hundreds, fifties and tens towards the Land given to them by their God. The men at Qumran could easily imagine themselves as being outside the land of Canaan and in preparation for its repossession when the time was fulfilled.

They also recalled in their writings the words from Isaiah, 'In the wilderness prepare the Lord's way,' regarding them as a summons which they had obeyed by coming here. The Hebrew word translated 'wilderness' is ᶜ*Arabah*, which designates this part of the Jordan rift valley.[2] The life of the men of

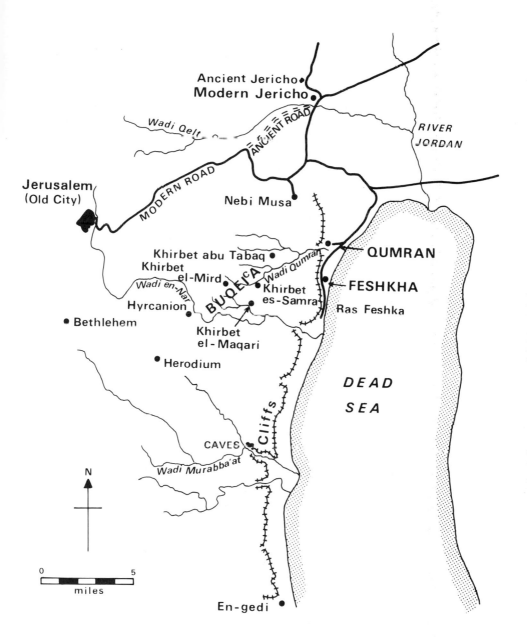

Map 1   This map shows the location of Qumran relative to Jerusalem, Jericho and Bethlehem, and includes the Buqei'a sites which are possibly to be identified with the cities of Joshua (see pp. 36–39).

Qumran was indeed a preparation, in their view, for the Lord's way, for the return from exile, both theirs and Israel's as they saw it, to true possession of the Land of Israel.

The region has other biblical associations, some of which the men of Qumran may have taken to heart. The Buqei'a may well be the Vale of Achor, the burial place of Achan whose disobedience hampered the conquest of Ai (Joshua 7:26). The wilderness of Judaea, which separated the men of Qumran from the Jerusalem whose society they so despised, was once the refuge of David fleeing from Saul. (It was also the place, so tradition affirms, of the temptation of Jesus, who lived in their day, but of whom the men of Qumran probably never heard. Or did they?) Nor is Qumran very far from the traditional place of the baptism of Jesus by John – a figure whom several scholars have suspected of having some association with its occupants.

Notes

1. This is often stated quite categorically, and is by and large correct. But at the beginning of this century Dr. E. W. G. Masterman did record observing small fish swimming in the Dead Sea near the Feshka springs – where, perhaps, the salt content of the water was below the sea's average.
2. Deuteronomy 3:17 refers to the Dead Sea as the Sea of the Arabah.

2

The Scrolls

If the setting of Qumran is remarkable, the ruins themselves are not. Qumran is not a great *tell* such as attracted the pioneers of modern archaeology from the turn of the century. Its name *Khirbet Qumran* ('ruins of Qumran') was borrowed from the wadi beside which it stood. It could simply have remained unexcavated to this day but for the remarkable discovery which took place just over thirty years ago. The chance finding of the Dead Sea Scrolls is one of the few great archaeological discoveries to have excited public imagination and interest.

The story of this discovery exists in many forms. Today, it is unlikely that we shall be able to reconstruct the exact course of events. The following version is rather less dramatic than some, but may be as close to the truth as we can reach.

The discovery was made some time during the winter of 1946–7. Three cousins belonging to the Beduin tribe of the Ta꜄amireh were watering their flocks of sheep and goats at ꜄Ain Feshkha. During such exercises one of the three, called Jum꜄a, liked to explore the caves which dotted the cliffs in the area hoping one day to find a cache of gold.

To the north of ꜄Ain Feshkha there are several hundred caves, and having wandered in this direction with his flocks, Jum꜄a was intrigued by a pair of openings, one above the other, in the cliff above him (Plate 2). On throwing a small rock into the lower opening, he heard a strange sound. He called to his companions and scrambled with them up to the openings, but since it was already growing dark by the time they reached there, the three of them agreed that they should investigate on the day after next, because on the following day they had to take their flocks back to ꜄Ain Feshkha. By the following evening they had watered their flocks and were once again encamped below the openings, ready to continue their exploration on the next morning.

Credit for discovering the Scrolls has been given to the youngest of the three cousins, Muhammad, nicknamed 'the wolf'. An enthusiastic teenager, he decided not to wait for his two companions, but left early in the morning and climbed alone to the spot. With some difficulty, he managed to squeeze himself through the upper opening. Once his eyes had become accustomed to the gloom, he saw that the floor was covered with broken earthenware. Then his glance fell upon a row of about ten jars, two to three feet high, stacked against the walls. All but two of these jars turned out to be empty; one of these two was full of earth, but from the other Muhammad extracted two bundles wrapped in linen, and one leather roll (Plate 19).

Not surprisingly, Muhammad's two cousins greeted his return with disapproval. Not only had he gone off without them, but he had failed to find any gold and could present only these three dirty bundles; for when the linen was unwrapped, the contents had turned out to be two more leather rolls. Later the three rolls, which appeared to be covered with writing in a strange script, were carried back to the main Ta'amireh centre near Bethlehem, where they were shown around and left for much of the time in a bag hanging from a tentpole. Eventually the disappointed treasure hunters arrived in Bethlehem, a town which had a number of dealers in legal and illegal traffic of various kinds. After several weeks of abortive negotiations with several of these, they left their find with a cobbler-cum-dealer known as Kando.

The events of the following months involved complicated dealings and further visits to the caves. Those concerned in these activities have naturally exercised some reticence over the details, but it seems that four more scrolls were brought back to Bethlehem; it is assumed that these were also found in the same cave as the first three. The total hoard of scrolls was then disposed of in two lots; four scrolls went to the Metropolitan of the Syrian Orthodox Church in Jerusalem, and three to Professor Eliezer Sukenik of the Hebrew University, also in Jerusalem. For his four scrolls the Metropolitan, Mar Yeshue Samuel, paid £24. He had no idea of their antiquity or value, but hoped that they might prove to be a good investment. Professor Sukenik, on the other hand, already had a shrewd idea of their significance. He recognised the writing on the scrolls as Hebrew and believed them to be both ancient and authentic; but he was not to disclose his opinions for some time.

It was in February of 1948, six months after he had acquired them, and after several disappointing assessments from various quarters, that Mar Samuel had his scrolls sent along to the American School of Oriental Research (now the Albright Institute) near the Old City. The Acting Director, John Trever, was shown two scrolls wrapped in newspaper. Although no expert in palaeography, Trever soon suspected that these scrolls, if authentic, might be about two thousand years old, and he immediately arranged to photograph them. For two months Trever, his colleague William Brownlee and, on his return, the Director, Millar Burrows, worked on the scrolls

Plate 2   Cave 1, the site of the original discovery. Originally it
possessed two small entrances which were enlarged into one by
the 'official' excavators a few years later.

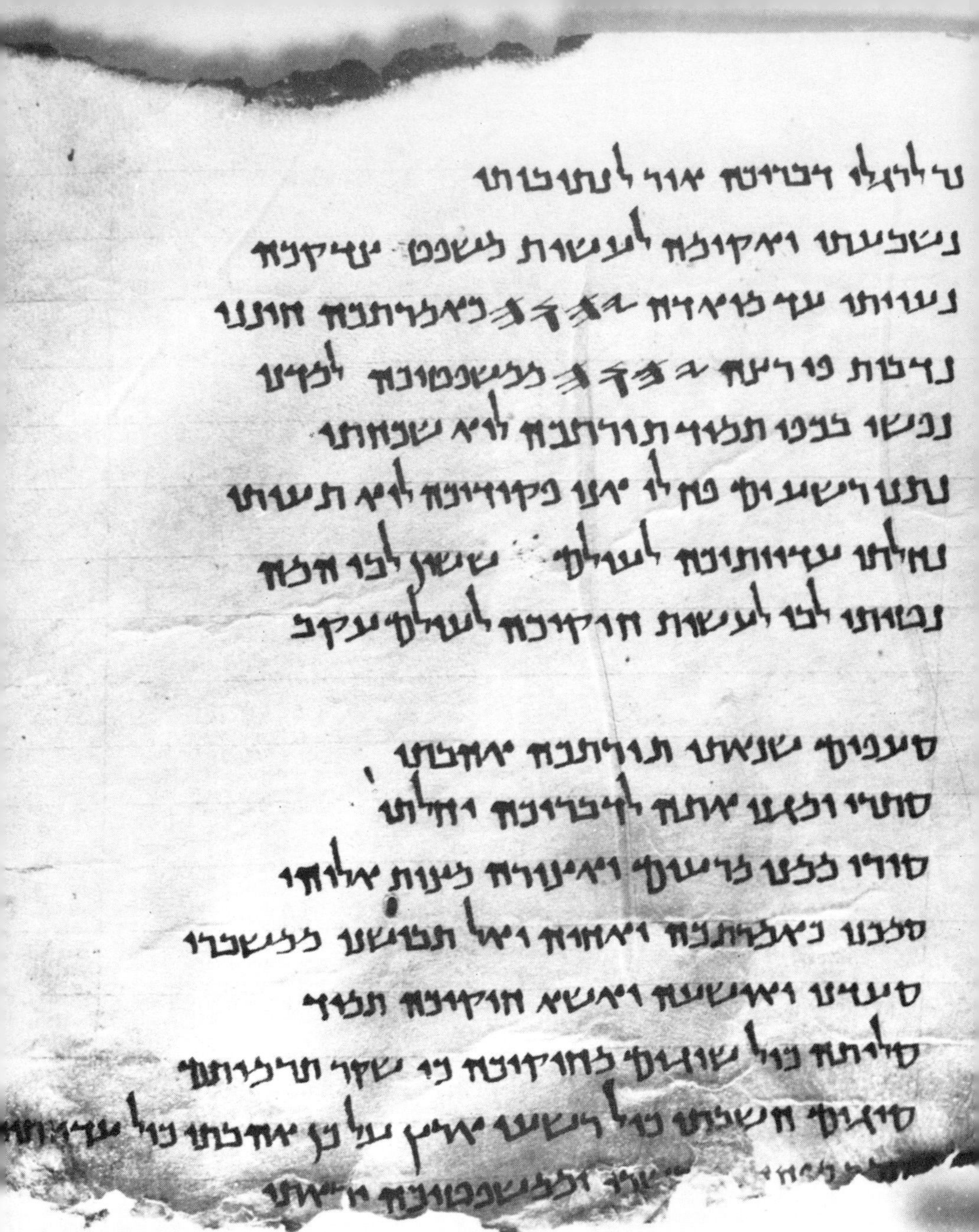

ע לולי דבירות אור כרות לעבעבע

נשבעתי ויאקובח לעשות משבת יעקקן

נעיותי עד כרירת �—⌐ כאכנרתכח חונו

נרבת פירעד ⌐ ⌐ בכשכבטוכח לבדע

נגשו בבנו תבגרי תורתבח לוא שכאתו

נתגרישעגוס פן לי ירע בכוריכוח לוא ת שוגו

נחלתו עגיוותותכח לעגלתו שטאן לבו הכח

נכוותו לבו לעשות חוקיכוח לעגלתו עקב

ט עגפוטס שגאשתו תורתכבח יראבטעו

סוטיי וכגגו אתתו לירבירכח יחלתו

סורדו כבבו כרישעף ויאיעוריח בעות יאלוחי

סככנו כאברותכח ויאחוו ואל תבושעו בכשכרו

ט עטעו ואישעטעו ויאשא חוקכמח תבדר

סליתתו כול שוגוף בחוקידוטה כי שקר תירכותער

סיגופ חשבטו טול רשעע יארק על כן יאהבתו כול עגיוותע

שרו דבבעכבוטכח יראע

בלתחד עשו לאמריתכנת לאמרו כתו תכחכען
כו עשותנו כנאמרו בקומטור חסדיכנח לוא שנחתו
כמה ולנו עבדיכנח כתו תענוח ברוורנו כשמ
כרו לו וודיתך שוחת אשר לוא כתחרתכנח
כול כעוותוכנח יכטנט שקורדינוו עוורנו
נכעכו כלנו נאמין ראנו לוא עוכתו פקודיכנח
כחסדיכנח חונו ראשוטורוח עויות טוכח

לעולם ... דכרנח נעכ כשמים
לידו וודו אכמטוכנח נונגתח ארטן ותעכדו
לכשפטויכנח עכדו חיוקי כו וכול עכדיוכנח
לוו ותורתכנח שעעשוען או אכקטו כעוונו
לעולם לוא אשכנח פקודיכנח כו ככה חווחנו
לכח אנו חוושועענו כו כקודיוכנח דרושתו
לוקקו רשעום לאכרנו עדוותונח צ תכונן
לעכל תכלח ראותח קץ רחכח כעעונב מודדח

against the background of a rapidly deteriorating political situation. The end of the British mandate in Palestine was imminent, and there was no one who doubted that war between Jews and Arabs would follow. But the Americans persuaded Mar Samuel to give them the rights to publish the scrolls, and on 11th April, 1948 the news of the Dead Sea Scrolls was broken. A fortnight later Sukenik announced the acquisition of his scrolls by the Hebrew University, on 15th May the war began in Palestine.

Mar Samuel and his scrolls left Jerusalem by different routes, and made their way to the United States. Meanwhile, during truces in the war, further visits to the cave were made, and more manuscripts came to light. Some of these were acquired by the Palestine Archaeological Museum. By this time, therefore, the contents of the manuscript cave were partly in Jerusalem and partly in the United States, and were distributed among three owners. Following such initial treatment, the scrolls were due for a more tranquil passage. After the ceasefire in Palestine, an official survey under the auspices of the Jordanian Department of Antiquities located the cave and the first fully legal transfer of its contents, to the Palestine Archaeological Museum in Jerusalem, took place. The same Museum also made further purchases of material in the possession of Kando. At this stage, however, the Museum may justifiably have felt rather like a dog begging for scraps after the table had been largely cleared.

In the United States, Mar Samuel had anxiously been seeking a purchaser for his scrolls in order to raise money for his community, and he finally succeeded in disposing of them for $250,000 to an anonymous buyer which turned out to be the State of Israel. This transaction took place in July 1954, by which time three of these scrolls had already been fully published, setting a fine example of scholarly efficiency and alacrity (which has subsequently

Plate 3   Two columns from the Cave 11 Psalms Scroll. The text here is Psalm 119:82–120. This is an acrostic psalm, divided into stanzas of eight lines, each one of which begins with the same letter of the Hebrew alphabet. The stanzas shown feature the letters k, l (m is lost at the foot of the right-hand column), n and s.

Notice in the third and fourth lines of the left-hand column the group of four letters in a different script. These form the divine name (YHWH) which out of reverence is written in the ancient Hebrew script used by the Israelites before they adopted the present script after the Exile (6th century BC).

26

been largely ignored!). In the spring of 1955 the Hebrew University's scrolls acquired by Sukenik (who had recently died) were also published and the Palestine Archaeological Museum followed shortly afterwards with its own material. Finally, the one remaining scroll from what was now called Qumran Cave I was published in 1956 by the Israeli scholars N. Avigad and Y. Yadin (for details, see the notes at the end of this chapter).

By this time, full excavations of the ruins of Qumran had commenced, and further caves containing scrolls had multiplied the amount of manuscript material. We shall pick up this thread presently. However, the story of the scrolls was by no means yet finished. In 1967 Israel occupied the West Bank and reunited all the scrolls then in Palestine under the single roof of the Shrine of the Book in Jerusalem. The work of editing the thousands of fragments, begun by an international team at the Palestine Archaeological Museum, continues and at the present rate will continue for a long time yet.

In 1978, one more major manuscript, the *Temple Scroll*, was published in full for the first time. It is the longest of all the Dead Sea Scrolls, measuring 28 feet in length, and it was first heard of in 1960. The famous Israeli archaeologist and scholar Yigael Yadin, the son of Eliezer Sukenik, acquired it from Kando in 1967 in circumstances about which one may only speculate. But we must be enormously thankful that this very valuable scroll was rescued; it had been hidden in a shoebox under a tile floor and wrapped in layers of paper, towelling and cellophane, and beside it was a cigar box which contained fragments and larger chunks of leather which had detached themselves from the scroll. Concerning other casualties of this process of 'safe keeping' and other vicissitudes we can only guess. Under the circumstances we ought perhaps to be grateful that what we do have has survived.

The story of the scrolls is even now not quite over. Numerous fragments remain to be sorted, identified and published, though it is unlikely that they will provide us with any more surprises. Yet even today rumours circulate of scrolls long since recovered but still hoarded. The story of the scrolls is bizarre enough to make such improbabilities both appealing and, at first glance, plausible. But such rumours appear to be much more the product of wishful thinking than informed speculation.

Notes on the Scrolls

Editions

The definitive editions of the Cave 1 scrolls referred to in this section are,
a) the scrolls acquired by Mar Samuel (St. Mark's Monastery),
    M. Burrows, J. C. Trever, W. H. Brownlee, *The Dead Sea Scrolls of St. Mark's Monastery*, American Schools of Oriental Research, New Haven, 1950–1, containing in vol. I a scroll of Isaiah (1QIs^a) and a commentary on Habakkuk (1QHab); and in vol. II the sectarian *Manual of Discipline* (or *Community Rule* as it is more frequently called) (1QS); N. Avigad, Y. Yadin, *A Genesis Apocryphon*, Magnes Press, Jerusalem, 1965, containing a retelling of Genesis from Noah to Abraham (1QGenAp);
b) the scrolls acquired by E. L. Sukenik for the Hebrew University,
    E. L. Sukenik, *The Dead Sea Scrolls of the Hebrew University*, Bialik, Jerusalem, 1955 (appeared in Hebrew in 1954) containing a second scroll of Isaiah (1QIs^b), the sectarian *War Rule* (1QM) and a collection of sectarian thanksgiving Hymns (1QH);
c) the fragments acquired by the Palestine Archaeological Museum,
    D. Barthélemy, J. T. Milik, *Discoveries in the Judaean Desert I: Qumran Cave 1*, Clarendon Press, Oxford, 1955 (including a description of the find, the cave and all its remaining contents).

Standard Abbreviations

A standard system of abbreviation for all the Qumran scrolls has been established, which consists of the following components,
1. the origin of the manuscript (1Q – 11Q = Qumran Caves 1–11);
2. the genre of the work (where appropriate), p = pesher (commentary), t = targum (Aramaic translation);
3. the title of the work, usually first letter or letters of the Hebrew designation, e.g. S = *serekh* (rule), M = *milḥamah* (war), H = *hodayot* (thanksgiving hymns);
4. where more than one fragment or copy of the same text exist, they are distinguished by a, b, c, d, etc.

One work of Qumran origin was first discovered in a Cairo synagogue at the end of the last century. Known as the *Zadokite Fragments* or *Damascus Rule*, its standard abbreviation is C (Cairo) D (Damascus). Fragments of this work which come from the Qumran caves are designated e.g. 6QD. Manuscripts and fragments without a title are given a number, e.g. the so-called *Copper Scroll* is 3Q15.

Bibliography

The most up-to-date list of all Qumran documents published is J. Fitzmyer, *The Dead Sea Scrolls. Major Publications and Tools for Study*, Scholars Press, Missoula, second edition, 1977, and the best and most recent introduction of the scrolls is G. Vermes, *The Dead Sea Scrolls. Qumran in Perspective*, Collins, London, 1977.

The best means of access to nearly all the texts in English is again provided by G. Vermes, *The Dead Sea Scrolls in English*, Penguin, second edition, 1975, although unfortunately the text gives only columns and not lines which impairs its value as a guide to study. For this reason the student may find useful A. Dupont-Sommer, *The Essene Writings from Qumran*, Blackwell, Oxford, 1961, which provides a translation of the main scrolls with introduction and notes. Vermes was able to include an introduction to and a translation of a few lines of the *Temple Scroll* (11QT); the definitive edition in Hebrew was published by the Israel Exploration Society, Jerusalem in 1978. The English edition is still awaited but translations in French and German are available.

Versions of the discovery of the scrolls are numerous and conflicting. The most reliable is probably John C. Trever, *The Dead Sea Scrolls: A Personal Account*, Eerdmans, Grand Rapids, 1977. Other accounts from those closely involved in the events or their aftermath are G. Lankester Harding, Director of the Jordanian Department of Antiquities at the time of the discoveries, in *Discoveries in the Judaean Desert I*, pp. 1–7, Millar Burrows in *The Dead Sea Scrolls*, New York, 1955 (reprinted, Baker, Grand Rapids, 1978), pp. 3–69; Frank M. Cross, Jr. (who was a member of the team of excavators and editors), *The Ancient Library of Qumran*, Duckworth, London, 1958, pp. 1–23; J. T. Milik (also one of the team of excavators and editors), *Ten Years of Discovery in the Judaean Wilderness*, S.C.M. Press, London, 1959, pp. 11–19; John Allegro, *The Dead Sea Scrolls, A Re-appraisal*, Penguin, second edition, 1964, pp. 17–36. It is also worth looking at numbers of *B.A.S.O.R.* from April 1948 onwards to read the first release of news about the find and the discussion which this and further developments provoked.

3

Uncovering the City

The ruins of Qumran are just over half a mile to the south of the cave where the manuscripts were first found. All that was visible at that time were a few piles of stones, a cistern, some traces of an aqueduct system near the wadi and a rather extensive cemetery covering the eastern part of the outcrop and stretching down to the coastal plain. Several eminent travellers in the nineteenth and early twentieth centuries had visited and described these remains. F. de Saulcy, in 1861, suggested that they were the remains of the biblical city of Gomorrah.

In 1873 C. Clermont-Ganneau, another Frenchman, made a brief survey of the ruins, and excavated one of the tombs in the cemetery, concluding that the site was insignificant. Between 1902 and 1913 Dr. E. W. G. Masterman, commissioned by the Palestine Exploration Fund to measure the level of the Dead Sea at ꜥAin Feshkha, took the opportunity to explore the surrounding region. He described the tombs and the aqueduct at Qumran, but drew no conclusions. In 1914 G. Dalman, who had recently visited the ruins, declared that they were the remains of a Roman fort, and in 1938 M. Noth proposed to identify the site with the biblical City of Salt mentioned in a list of Judaean towns in Joshua 15:61–2. Noth later withdrew his suggestion; but it has turned out that he was quite probably correct, and Dalman too. But both were still far from the whole truth.

It is as if Qumran was destined to keep its secrets. For even after the whereabouts of the scroll cave had been officially ascertained by a Jordanian expedition in 1949, its connection with Qumran was dismissed. The Director of the Jordanian Department of Antiquities, G. Lankester Harding, and Fr. Roland de Vaux of the École Biblique in Jerusalem, who jointly conducted the official examination of the cave, concluded from a brief survey of the Qumran ruins that they were the remains of a Roman fort from the third or fourth century AD, whereas the manuscripts and the pottery from the cave were (wrongly) placed in the second century BC. But as the contents of the scrolls became more widely known, there grew a demand from scholars on all sides that the Qumran ruins should be reinvestigated. Several experts had realised that the scrolls could well belong to a Jewish sect which, according

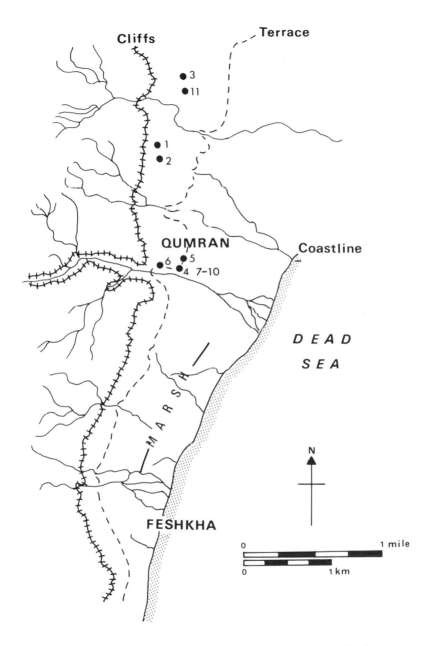

Cliffs

Terrace

●3
●11

●1
●2

QUMRAN

Coastline

●6 ●5
●4 7-10

DEAD

SEA

MARSH

N

FESHKHA

0   1 mile

0   1 km

Map 2   This map of the Qumran region illustrates the topographical features. The numbers refer to the 11 caves which contained manuscripts.

to the Roman writer Pliny the Elder, had a settlement near the shore of the Dead Sea. In November 1951, therefore, Harding and de Vaux conducted a preliminary excavation of the Qumran ruins, under the auspices of the Jordanian Department of Antiquities, the École Biblique and the Palestine Archaeological Museum (also known as the Rockefeller Museum), and almost immediately it became clear that the cave and the ruins were after all connected. Identical pottery types came to light, including a 'scroll jar', and among the coins unearthed were some which dated from the first century AD and earlier. This dating corresponded with the period to which the palaeographers – not without protests from those who still regarded the finds as a hoax – were assigning the manuscripts. It became clear that Qumran was, after all, the home of the community which had written the scrolls.

Excavations were interrupted by news of more sensations. Another hoard of manuscripts was in the possession of the Beduin, and the origin of the finds was traced to the Wadi Murabba'at, twelve miles south west of Qumran (see map p. 19). Although of great importance, these manuscripts turned out to have no connection with the discoveries at Qumran, but the excavations were abandoned as de Vaux scurried off in pursuit of the new finds. Not so the Beduin explorers! With the archaeologists away and aware of the financial rewards which manuscript discoveries could bring them, they again turned their attention to the region of their original finds. Close to the first cave they discovered a second. It had apparently occurred to no one but the Beduin that the first cave might not be an isolated instance. The discovery of Cave 2 brought back the archaeologists and provoked a full-scale official search of all caves in the cliffs, extending over a stretch of five miles. This search revealed Cave 3, the most northerly of the caves which yielded manuscripts, and its prize was two scrolls which caused a great stir (Plates 22, 23). They were both made of copper, and formed a single manuscript. Although the contents were not published until 1956 it had become clear from an early stage that they had to do with hidden treasure – as it turned out, sixty treasure stores and their locations. Among the speculations was the suggestion that this list referred to the temple treasures smuggled from Jerusalem during the war of AD 66–70 with the Romans. But despite more than one expedition in search of this lost wealth nothing turned up. It is now widely suspected that not only the hiding places but the treasures themselves are legendary. If this is the case, it is not the only product of the imagination to emerge from the scrolls. Fact and fantasy seem to have intermingled at Qumran, and drawing the line between them is not an easy task for the modern investigator. How far the men of Qumran themselves drew a line is not always easy to discover.

Responding to the discovery of Cave 3 as if to a challenge, the Beduin

Plate 4   The Wadi Qumran seen from the coastal plain. The edge of the Qumran outcrop is to the right, and at the bottom right-hand corner is Cave 4 which yielded the richest of the manuscript hoards.

brought to Jerusalem, in the next six months, more manuscripts from an unidentified cave in the Naḥal Ḥever south of En-gedi, and from Khirbet el Mird, five miles west of Qumran (see map p. 19). The Beduin scroll-hunt was undoubtedly being conducted on a massive scale, and it bore fruit yet again at Qumran. For while they had carefully surveyed all the caves in the cliffs, the archaeologists had ignored those in the limestone terrace and the outcrop on which the Qumran ruins stood. Right under their noses, the Beduin excavators came across the biggest haul of all, from Cave 4 on the southern edge of the outcrop and easily visible from the bed of the Wadi Qumran (Plate 4). This cave proved to contain the remains of some four hundred manuscripts. The archaeologists once again moved in to complete the excavation, and also discovered, close to it, Cave 5. Cave 6 was traced by the Beduin, near the waterfall of the Wadi Qumran.

These events took place between February and September 1952. It was not until February 1953 that the second season of excavations commenced at the Qumran ruins. By now, of course, the scale of the settlement and its literary remains had become much clearer. No more manuscript caves were found until the fourth season in 1955, when numbers 7–10 were revealed on the eastern slope of the Qumran outcrop. The contents of these caves, whose discovery is credited to the official excavators, did not prove to be particularly important. But the eleventh cave, a mile north of Qumran and close to Cave 3, was found and emptied by the Beduin who were able subsequently to sell their spoils to the officials. The final score in cave discovery was therefore six to the official parties and five to the Beduin. The trade in manuscripts was rather brisk as the Beduin had much to sell. They exhausted the funds of the various Jordanian institutions, and foreign institutions were invited to purchase lots on the condition that the texts remained at the Palestine Archaeological Museum for editing. An official standard price was set for manuscripts, roughly £1 per square centimetre of written surface. This policy succeeded in keeping the scrolls together and avoided many other dangers which would otherwise have threatened their preservation. In addition, de Vaux employed some of the Taʿamireh Beduin as workmen in the official excavations of Qumran. Few would deny that they had earned it!

It must be made clear that the numbered caves to which we have just referred represent only those in which manuscript material was found. Numerous other caves in the vicinity yielded other finds. The caves in the cliffs, all of which were natural cavities, included forty from which pottery and other objects were recovered, twenty-six containing pottery identical with that found in the Qumran ruins – mainly jugs, bowls and lamps. From this it seemed that the caves had been inhabited, usually by individuals who were presumably members of the Qumran community; a few caves were apparently used as stores. The density of occupation of these caves increased in the vicinity of Qumran, and one interesting feature of the distribution is that the inhabited caves tend to form groups separated by stretches where no occupied caves occur. De Vaux has suggested that this may simply be due to variations of contour in the terrain or ease of access, but it may be rather that the community of Qumran was divided into groups; there is some evidence in the scrolls for such an organisation.

The caves in the terrace and the outcrop, by contrast, are all artificial. Of these, Cave 4 is the most interesting. It was densely packed with scrolls, stored without jars in such a way as to suggest that its contents were hastily concealed. Its position makes it extremely difficult to enter, and the excavators had to cut steps in the side of the terrace to gain access. It has been suggested that this cave housed the community library, but this accounts for neither the disarray of the contents nor the traces of human habitation.

A total of some thirty caves, extending over two miles north and south of Qumran, seems to have been occupied at the same time as the ruins. Together with the ruins, these give a picture of a settlement consisting of a community centre (Qumran) used by people who actually dwelt either in the caves or in tents or huts. Five wooden posts, two of them forked at the end, were found hidden in a crevice together with fragments of pottery which, de Vaux suggests, are the remains of the supporting posts of a tent or hut and the utensils used in it. As we shall see, no living quarters have been identified in what remains of the Qumran buildings themselves. Unless, then, we are able to conceive of a city without houses, we ought to include the area containing the inhabited caves within the 'city limits' of Qumran.

Qumran was excavated in five seasons, in 1951 and 1953–6. A further season of excavation in 1958 took place at the associated site of ʿAin Feshkha which, it emerged, also belonged to the Qumran complex. The progress of all the excavations was fully and promptly reported in the *Revue Biblique*, the journal of the École Biblique, and a summary of the findings was issued in 1961 (in French) by the Oxford University Press, being in fact the text of the 1959 Schweich Lectures delivered by de Vaux at the British Academy. In 1972 a revised text was translated into English and it remains the definitive account of the work done and of the author's considered conclusions. Despite one or two lapses during the early stages of excavation which we have already noted, Roland de Vaux's work at Qumran was that of a brilliant scholar and a thoroughly competent archaeologist. He combined to an unusual degree the gifts of imagination and common-sense. In presenting the results of the excavations at Qumran, I make no apology for relying, in common with many other scholars, almost exclusively on de Vaux's reports; and where I disagree it is with great caution.

The excavations at Qumran provided evidence of five main phases of occupation. The three phases with which we are chiefly concerned, and with which the scrolls are linked, fall between the middle of the second century BC and AD 68: these represent an almost continuous occupation of Qumran by a Jewish sectarian community, and de Vaux designates them period Ia, period Ib and period II. Several centuries earlier is the initial phase of occupation, which de Vaux calls the Israelite period, and there is a brief phase of occupation after AD 68 by Roman forces, which de Vaux designates period III. The history of occupation of Qumran as reconstructed by the archaeological excavations is therefore relatively straightforward, and also relatively reliable, with a greater degree of absolute dating than is usually the case with the major cities of the biblical world.

The Israelite period

Although the outline of the Israelite remains has been obscured by later building, it can be roughly reconstructed; the foundations of some of the walls are on a lower level than walls assigned to the subsequent periods, and the location of sherds from the Iron Age II period (c. 1000–550 BC) also assists in their identification. There is a simple rectangular building (Plan 1) forming a courtyard with rooms along its eastern wall, and perhaps along other walls also. On the western side an outbuilding housed a large circular cistern which was apparently filled by drainage from the terrace and not from the wadi. This cistern is a useful Qumran landmark, since it remained in use throughout the successive periods of occupation. From the southeast corner of the building a wall ran in a southerly direction, and this feature may be an important clue in ascertaining the purpose of this ancient building.

The dating of the remains belonging to the Israelite period relies on both archaeological and biblical evidence. Apart from the indications given by the type of pottery, whose remains point quite clearly to this period, there was also found an ostracon on which were written letters in the old Hebrew script which was in use before the Babylonian exile (586–538 BC) and a jar-handle inscribed 'to (or, of) the king'. This belongs to a type well-known from other sites in Israel (such as Lachish), and points, with the other evidence, to the eighth or seventh centuries BC. The ashes which were consistently found with the Israelite sherds suggest a violent destruction of Israelite Qumran which it is tempting to identify with one or other of the Babylonian invasions of Judah which culminated in the exile.

Further light on this Israelite foundation is cast by the results of a survey which two members of de Vaux's team, Frank M. Cross, Jr. and J. T.

THE ISRAELITE PERIOD

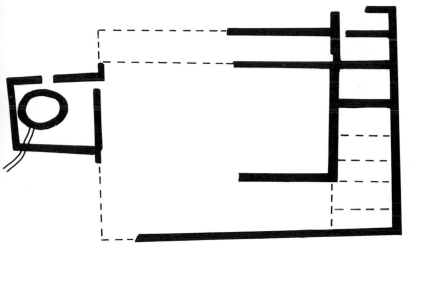

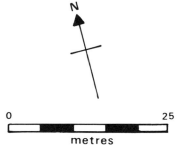

N

0   25

metres

Plan 1   The Israelite Period. A simple enclosure surrounded by rooms, with a single round cistern adjoining the western wall.

Milik, undertook during the 1955 season. Their attention had been drawn to three other sites, possibly from the same period, located in the Buqeiʿa close to Qumran. These were called Khirbet abu Tabaq, Khirbet es-Samra and Khirbet el-Maqari (see map p. 19). At each of these three sites the survey revealed a structure whose plan was similar if not identical to that postulated for Israelite Qumran – rectangular buildings, cisterns and enclosure walls. Towers and dams were among features found here but not present at Qumran. All the sites were datable to Iron II, the sherds being of the same type as those of Qumran.

Cross and Milik drew the conclusion that all these sites, including Qumran, were probably built at the same period and for an identical purpose. Following the lead given by Noth (see above, p. 30) they referred to the list of Judaean cities mentioned in Joshua 15: 61–2,

> and in the desert Beth-Arabah, Middin and Sekakah and Nibshan and the City of Salt and En-gedi, six cities and their estates.

En-gedi is about twenty miles south of Qumran; Beth-Arabah is perhaps near the present ʿAin el-Gharabeh, just south-east of Jericho. It could be, Cross and Milik suggested, that the cities in the biblical list are named from north to south, and that Middin, Sekakah and Nibshan are the three Buqeiʿa sites, respectively Khirbet abu Tabaq, Khirbet es-Samra and Khirbet al-Maqari, with Qumran as the 'City of Salt' – an appropriate enough name for a settlement near the shore of the Sea of Salt. This suggestion was encouraged by the existence of an ancient track along the Wadi Qumran, linking the Qumran site with the Buqeiʿa. Although this track was used in the later periods of occupation at Qumran when the Buqeiʿa sites were apparently deserted, it might well have originally served to link four contemporary Israelite settlements.

Biblical scholars doubt, however, that the foundation of these four settlements could have occurred in the time of Joshua. The question, then, is, who did build them, why and when? A possible answer may be provided by two further biblical references. According to 2 Chronicles 17:12 Jehoshaphat, king of Judah (870–48) 'built in Judah fortresses and store-cities'. In 2 Chronicles 26:10 we read that also Uzziah, king of Judah (781–40) 'built towers in the wilderness and dug many cisterns'. Uzziah is also said to have 'loved the soil', perhaps implying that his towers and cisterns had an agricultural function. Jehoshaphat, on the other hand, apparently built for military purposes.

Of the two kings, therefore, Uzziah seems the more likely, and this is the conclusion to which de Vaux himself inclined. But some objections to the whole theory ought to be pointed out. The agricultural function of the

38

Buqei'a cities seems quite probable, for their system of dams, irrigation and walls looks to be too elaborate for purely military settlements. But did Israelite Qumran serve the same purpose? The value of the site, perched on a small plateau overlooking the Dead Sea and difficult of access, is considerable for a military settlement, but far from ideal, or even suitable, for agriculture. There is no cultivable land within the immediate vicinity. Perhaps Qumran *was*, after all, a defensive post, built to guard the agricultural sites in the Buqei'a from raiders.

Further difficulties remain, however. The *Copper Scroll* indeed mentions the name 'Sekaka' several times, both as a site and as a wadi. Almost certainly the wadi in question is the Wadi Qumran, but which site also bears the name? Both Khirbet es-Samra and Khirbet Qumran are located by the wadi and could have taken its name. According to Cross and Milik, 'Sekaka' will have been the ancient name of Khirbet es-Samra; and certainly Qumran, close to the Dead Sea, is more plausibly the 'City of Salt'. Besides, no other site in the vicinity has yet been uncovered which could reasonably be identified as the City of Salt. Nevertheless, more recently it was Qumran which took the name of the wadi. Furthermore, the Cross-Milik identifications suppose that the biblical list of cities enumerates them from north to south. A glance at the map on page 19 will show, however, that this sequence does not strictly fit the facts, for Qumran lies to the north of all the Buqei'a sites.

In addition to all this, another site of similar construction and date to the three Buqei'a sites has been excavated ten miles south of Qumran, near a spring called 'Ain el-Ghuweir. The excavator, P. Bar-Adon, wishes to identify this site with one of the cities of Joshua 15, and proposes that all of the places in the list originally stood by the shore of the Dead Sea. According to this theory, Qumran could well be 'Sekaka', and 'Ain el-Ghuweir the 'City of Salt'. With En-gedi as the final city on the list, it is true that the last three places would all be located beside the Dead Sea. But Bar-Adon's proposal leaves the location of the first three cities on the list unknown.

The Cross-Milik theory, which is at present widely accepted, does appear the more likely. But perhaps a small modification is required, in view of the discovery of the remains of a building about half a mile south of Qumran. It was only during the last months of excavation, in 1956, that the outline of the building was discerned from the top of the cliffs. Excavations revealed a larger but simpler version of the Israelite building at Qumran. The pottery it contained led de Vaux to speculate that it may have been occupied a little earlier than Qumran. Its location is certainly better suited to agriculture, since it is adjacent to the area of the Dead Sea coastal plain irrigated by freshwater springs. From its eastern side a wall was traced running south for more than 500 yards, possibly bounding a farming estate. (This wall, also similar to the walls of the Buqeiʿa sites, continued in use during later periods.) De Vaux concluded that this newly-discovered building, dating from perhaps the ninth century BC, was later abandoned in favour of Qumran. Supposing this speculation to be correct, is it this site which originally bore the name 'City of Salt'? The problem of identifying Israelite Qumran may well be more difficult than many scholars are willing to concede; it goes without saying that to identify Qumran with a named biblical city provides the archaeologist, both professional and amateur, with a great deal of satisfaction. But, as de Vaux with his typical caution remarked, 'The west bank of the Dead Sea was more thickly populated than we have been accustomed to imagine' (*A.D.D.S.* pp. 89–90), and we may need to revise our conclusions in the event of future discoveries in the area.

Period Ia

From the middle of the second century BC until AD 68, with a break at the end of the first century BC, Qumran was occupied by the community which produced the scrolls. This occupation is represented at Qumran by three periods, labelled by de Vaux Ia, Ib and II. It is these periods with which we are chiefly concerned. A fairly brief account of the archaeological data pertaining to these periods follows, which will be augmented later by a fuller description of the way of life practised by the community.

A comparison of the plan of period Ia with that of the Israelite period (Plans 1, 2) shows the extent to which the more recent phase of building developed the existing remains. The great circular cistern (1) was re-used, two rectangular cisterns (2–3) were constructed beside it, and a decantation basin (4) was added which served all three cisterns. From this we can learn that the new inhabitants required more water than their predecessors, and we shall have reason to suspect that this was not simply because of increased numbers. The water continued to be collected simply by drainage from the terrace, but two channels were dug to the north and south of the building (5–6) in order to enlarge the catchment area. Some small rooms whose purpose is uncertain, were also built round the cisterns (7–9), and in the eastern part two potter's kilns were installed side by side (10–11).

There is little more that we can reconstruct from the remains of this period, because in the following period, Ib, a considerable rebuilding took place which obliterated most of the traces of the earlier period. Pottery associated with Ia is indistinguishable from that of Ib, and although a few silver coins dating from BC 130 may belong to Ia we cannot be very sure. Silver coins remained in circulation for much longer than bronze coins. Even if these do belong to Ia, they can give us no precise idea of when period Ia

PERIOD 1a.

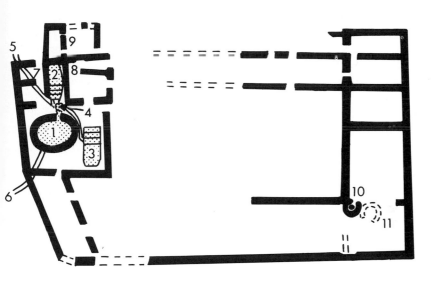
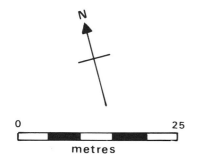

N

0   25

metres

Plan 2   Period Ia. The major development here is the addition of two
rectangular cisterns alongside the Israelite round one, with an
additional inlet channel for collecting the water.

commenced. Indeed, this question can best be tackled on the evidence of the scrolls themselves rather than from archaeological data. It can be deduced from the remains of Ia, however, that the inhabitants at this period were not numerous; perhaps a few dozen or so. It also seems that this small settlement did not last for more than a few decades at most. Working back from the commencement of period Ib, which we can determine rather more accurately, we can say on the basis of the archaeological evidence only that in the second half the second century BC or just possibly the very beginning of the first century, a small group of persons rebuilt on a modest scale the ruins of a building abandoned for over three hundred years. While for historians of the Qumran community this first stage is a most important as well as problematic one, it is unfortunately the least well attested archaeologically of all the phases of occupation by the community.

Period Ib

Period Ib is marked not by a break in occupation but by a sudden and very considerable expansion of the existing facilities, undoubtedly occasioned by an increase in the size of the community, of perhaps the order of three or four times the original total. Not only is the number of buildings increased, but their scope and function are also enlarged; many new activities were now pursued in what had become more or less a self-sufficient settlement. The activity which initiated this period brought the Qumran buildings to virtually their definitive form, and this is the proper point at which to conduct as it were a guided tour of the establishment (Plan 3).

We approach Qumran, as the ancient visitor would have done, from the north or north-east. Our first sight of the settlement is the tower which stands at the north-west corner of the main block and overlooks the main entrance to Qumran (2). This structure was built not simply as a watchtower, from which the approach of visitors (friendly or otherwise) could be observed over a considerable distance, but also with defensive needs in mind. For there is no entrance to the tower at ground level; to gain access you had to climb a staircase situated well inside the main block and tread a wooden gangway across to the tower. The storerooms which occupied its ground floor were reached by descending a spiral staircase inside the tower.

Passing through the main entrance adjacent to the tower, we find ourselves in a courtyard with a doorway to our left (3) which leads into the main corridor of the settlement. This corridor separates the main block on the east from the buildings which form a smaller block on the west (Plate 5). We find our way from the corridor into the main, eastern, block through one of two doorways set side by side. The first of these (5) leads via a short

PERIOD 1b: c. 103-31 BC

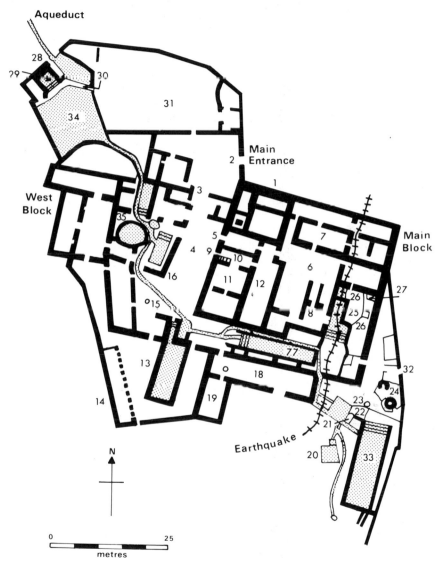

Plan 3   Period Ib, *c.* 103 – 31 BC. The building of the previous periods
has been enlarged and forms the main block, with a tower at its
north-west corner. A western block has developed round the
existing cisterns, and several more cisterns have been built
together with an elaborate water system.

passage into the central courtyard of the main block (6). The eastern end of this passage had once possessed a wooden door, whose iron nails were found lying on the paved floor. On the northern side of the courtyard were the kitchens (7), and in the south-east corner some small rooms where basins had once stood (8). According to some reconstructions, these formed part of a large and elaborate bath-house. The buildings on the western side of the courtyard, and possibly those on the eastern side also, were two storeys high.

The second of the two doorways from the central corridor led into a vestibule on the ground floor of the main block (10). This vestibule in turn gave access to two rooms, one of which (11) contained benches running along its walls and may therefore have been an assembly room of some kind. It also had recessed cupboards and a curious small niche in its northern wall which was accessible from both inside and outside. Hence the suggestion that it may have been a receptacle by means of which members in closed session within the room could be served with water or nourishment without being disturbed. The second room leading off from the vestibule (12) was larger than the first. Its original purpose is unclear, but what excited the excavators were the contents of the room above it which had fallen through the collapsed ceiling. The first floor of this part of the building was reached from a staircase in the south-west corner of the little vestibule which also, as has been mentioned, led via a gangway to the tower. The contents of the upper room which aroused so much interest consisted largely of pieces of mudbrick covered with smooth plaster. These pieces were carefully collected and sent to the Palestine Archaeological Museum for reassembly. The result of much painstaking labour became one of the most cherished exhibits in the Museum – a table about 16 feet long and 16 inches wide, but only 20 inches high and 7 inches wide at the base (Plate 20). It transpired, too, that the fragments belonged to more than one such table. In addition, the room was found to contain the remains of what had once been a low bench running along the inside of the eastern wall. Also recovered was a plastered platform or small table which was rimmed and had two shallow cavities on its surface.

Despite early doubts expressed from various quarters, the excavators were finally satisfied that this upper room was the place in which the Dead Sea scrolls had been written, and it was designated the 'scriptorium'. Confirmation of this was provided by the discovery of two inkwells containing dried ink, one made of earthenware and the other of bronze. How exactly the furniture in the room was employed is less certain. Most probably the scribes sat along the benches – or simply squatted on the floor – and wrote on the tables. But, as de Vaux himself confessed, this method of writing is unknown elsewhere until the second century AD. The customary method of

Plate 5   A view of the central corridor of the Qumran settlement taken from the tower and looking south. To the left is the main block, entered via the passage in the foreground. At the end of the corridor can be seen, from right to left, a cistern and the refectory, with the pantry (containing the stumps of two pillars) beyond.

writing was to sit with the material on the scribe's lap. Had the reconstructed table been stronger at the base, we should have assumed that the scribes of Qumran sat on the 'tables' and rested their feet on the 'benches'. There is also something of a mystery about the object with the two cavities. De Vaux suggested that it held water for washing the hands, which may have been regarded as necessary for scribes handling sacred manuscripts. But we cannot be certain that this custom was observed at Qumran, and in any case the object does not seem ideally designed for this purpose. Other possible uses must not be left out of consideration, such as cleaning pens or preparing skin for writing.

These uncertainties notwithstanding, the writing of manuscripts is the one activity which we can be absolutely certain to have been carried out at Qumran, and the identification of this room as the scriptorium effectively sealed the connection between the caves and the ruins, and thus understandably its discovery marked one of the high points of the excavation.

With this room our visit to the main block of the settlement is completed. Returning to the central corridor by either of the two doorways already mentioned, we see facing us beyond the corridor the remains of the original round cistern and the two rectangular cisterns which were later added. Quite possibly these would once have been covered with a palm thatch roof to reduce evaporation (Plate 11). Running south-east from these cisterns, the water channel led to another, large cistern at the southern end of the corridor (13). The rooms surrounding and to the west of the group of three cisterns were used for storage, since some of them were plastered, and also probably as workshops. The area in the south-west corner of this western block has been suggested as the site of the stables (14). Being so far from any of the main entrances to Qumran, it is perhaps not an ideal place for this suggested function, and the identification is far from certain. No doubt pack-animals were housed somewhere in the settlement, since the provisions stored in the rooms of this western block had to be brought from elsewhere, mainly from the Buqei'a and the Feshkha region.

Among these provisions was grain; and close to the water channel where it crosses the south-west corner of the central corridor (15) was a circular platform, with a groove cut in its surface, set on a paved area. This is where the millstones would have been set, the flour falling into the groove underneath (Plates 17, 18). The millstones themselves were unearthed a few yards to the south where they seem to have been thrown away as being of no further use by the Roman soldiers who occupied Qumran during period III. Just north of the mill was the baking oven (16); at least this is where it was situated in period II, when it was walled in (see Plan 4), and presumably it would always have been placed fairly close to the mill. From the ashes of

Plate 6   A general view of the potter's workshop, looking south. In the
foreground to the left is the large kiln. Just above the steps in
the foreground and slightly to the right is the site of the wheel
and beside it the basin for the clay. To the right of the
workshop the eastern end of the refectory can be seen, and to
the left, behind the wheel, the cistern which formed the end of
the water-system.

wooden beams and of palm-thatch left after the fire which brought period Ib to an end, it is clear that much of this western block was roofed, and may even have possessed a second storey as at least part of the main block did. As with the main block, too, we are unable to reconstruct the function of several of the rooms, but it seems that most of the routines of economic life at Qumran were centred on this part of the settlement.

At the southern end of the central corridor, in front of the big cistern which we have already mentioned (13), we turn to our left (towards the east, that is), and find ourselves facing yet another rectangular cistern built against the southern wall of the main block (17). To our right, across the water channel is the largest room at Qumran (Plate 5). During period Ib it had a doorway at the north-west corner, through which we now enter, and another doorway near the south-east corner, which led directly on to the terrace and offered a view down the coastal plain to Feshkha.

It is still noticeable that the floor of this room slopes towards this south-eastern corner and we should be right in thinking that this feature had something to do with drainage; just to the left of the north-west door by which we entered is a side-channel which runs from the main water channel into the room, and can be opened by means of a sluice. With great ease, therefore, the floor of this room could be washed out, the water simply running out on to the terrace. What sort of room would require such treatment? The answer was provided by the contents of an annexe adjoining the room to the south (19). This little room had been blocked off in period II but during Ib it was evidently connected with the larger room which it served. More than a thousand pieces of crockery – jars, jugs, beakers, dishes and bowls were found stacked here. This was no doubt a pantry, which meant that the larger room was the refectory: hence the need for frequent washing of the floor.

The refectory is conveniently situated away from the main working areas of the settlement but also – assuming our identifications to be correct – inconveniently distant from the kitchens in the north of the main block! However, we must understand that this room was built to accommodate most, if not all, of the members of the enlarged community of period Ib, and such a room will have needed to be built outside the main block, which was already standing in period Ia.

It appears from the scrolls that the community's meals – or some of them – were accompanied by religious ceremonies. Indeed, the meal itself was a religious ceremony. At the western end of the refectory, there is a circular paved area where – it is widely surmised – the priest who presided over the meal (and other ceremonies) probably stood. Since this room was the only room at Qumran apparently capable of accommodating all the members of

Plate 7   The large potter's kiln, looking northwest and towards the spot
from which plate 6 was taken. The aperture shown on both
plates was for kindling the fire; a higher aperture on the south
side of the kiln allowed the pottery to be placed above the fire.
Beyond the kiln the smaller kiln can be seen (see plate 8).

the community, it may have been used for occasions other than meals,
whenever all the members were required to be present.

The potter's workshop is situated nearby, and this can be reached by
turning left (towards the east) after leaving the refectory by the south-east
doorway. This workshop included a shallow plastered basin (20) in which
the clay was washed, using water from the channel which ran alongside the
north wall of the refectory before turning north along the east wall of the
main block. Next to this first basin was a pit where the washed clay was left

to mature (21) and a trough in which the final mixing took place (22) (Plate 6). The wheel itself stood in a stone-lined pit (23) with the potter seated on the edge, working the wheel with his feet (as some present-day Arab potters can still be seen to do). For firing the pottery there were two kilns inside the eastern wall of the settlement (24) (Plates 7, 8): these faced in opposite directions and hence, as de Vaux argued, could be used when the wind was either northerly or southerly. Although of different sizes, they are both of a similar construction, the interior divided into a lower and an upper chamber by a shelf on which the pieces were placed; the fire was lit below the shelf and the draught provided by the vent at the top. The fact that this single workshop apparently provided all of the pottery used at Qumran satisfactorily explains both the relative lack of variety in types and relative lack of development throughout periods I and II. (Some examples of Qumran pottery can be seen on Figure 3.) On the other hand, the pottery is similar enough to other forms of pottery from Palestine to allow significant comparison for dating purposes.

Our tour of the settlement ends with a look at the enclosure to the east of the main block. Here are two more cisterns with a shared decantation basin (25), and, to the east of these, a kind of small bathing area (26) with stone basins. Just north of this was a store-room (27) where several iron tools were found. This means either that there was a forge nearby, as de Vaux thinks, or that such tools, when not in use, were placed here by members of the community as they returned to the settlement after working on the Qumran estate.

This leads us to the question of the entrances to Qumran. We have so far mentioned only one, the main entrance to the north, beside the tower. But in fact the main areas in which the members of the community worked outside Qumran were to the west, in the Buqei'a vale above the cliffs, and to the south, around Feshkha on the Dead Sea coastal plain. An entrance on the north side of the settlement was clearly impractical for people returning from either of these directions. However, there was an entrance at the north-west corner, adjacent to the point where the aqueduct led into the buildings, and at the point where the track from the Buqei'a via the Wadi Qumran reached the buildings. That this was a main entrance for the members is indicated by the presence of a bath which would have been used before entering the settlement proper (Plate 16) (29). When this bathing was completed, the way into the buildings led along a bridge which crossed the aqueduct (30) and into the large outer courtyard to the north (31), and hence towards the main doorway beside the foot of the tower.

It is also quite likely that another entrance lay somewhere in the south-east corner, perhaps just north of the potter's kilns (32). Such an entrance

50

Plate 8   The small potter's kiln. The fire was lit in the lower chamber, and in the shelf above can be seen the flues through which the heat passed to the upper chamber which held the pottery.

would have served those approaching from the south. As we have noticed, there appear to have been bathing facilities in this area and a place for storing tools. Alternatively, an entrance may have lain between the cistern at the extreme south-eastern corner of Qumran and the boundary wall to the east of it (33). Unlike the north-western entrance, however, this entrance remains only a conjecture.

The water system has already been referred to several times during our

51

brief survey of the settlement. There can be no doubt that the provision of water was a matter of great importance at Qumran. The cisterns dominate the whole complex, large, deep and distributed over almost every part, linked by a water channel which in addition provided water in areas where it was constantly needed for pottery-making, laundering, cleaning, bathing, cooking, drinking and no doubt other industrial uses. It was fed only by the rainwater which once or twice every rainy season (roughly, in spring and autumn) poured in torrents down the Wadi Qumran. Some of this water was trapped in a natural basin from where it was drained off and carried by an aqueduct some 750 yards into the north-west corner of Qumran. For the first 100 yards, this aqueduct ran along the edge of the wadi, then it turned north and cut into the cliffs and passed through a tunnel. After emerging, it coursed down the side of the cliff and along the narrow neck which joins the Qumran outcrop to the main limestone terrace at the base of the cliffs. Before it reached the buildings, its flow was regulated by a sluice. Inside the settlement, it debouched into a large and shallow reservoir which acted as an initial decantation basin.

This aqueduct is a remarkable piece of engineering. Its course can for the most part still be clearly traced (Plates 14, 15). Indeed, it is possible to crawl through the tunnel, which measures on average three feet in height and just over two feet in width, and is ventilated by two shafts. In some places the original plaster which must have lined the entire course of the aqueduct can still be seen.

The water which now settled in the large reservoir was drawn off through the channel to the three cisterns in the western block (35), then to the cistern at the southern end, and turned east to feed the cistern between the main block and the refectory. At this point the channel passed north of the cistern and turned north at the corner of the main block to fill the two cisterns in the eastern enclosure. Finally, it reversed its direction and flowed south to fill the cistern in the south-east corner, passing the potter's workshop for the second time. Even after all these cisterns had been filled, there must have been an excess of water, for clearly discernible is an 'overflow channel' leading from the last-mentioned cistern on to the terrace.

We have now some idea of the scale, complexity and function of the installations at Qumran during period Ib. Our next task is to consider the dating of this period. Here we are fortunate in being able to utilise some fairly hard evidence. For the beginning of Ib an approximate date is indicated by both pottery types and coinage associate with the remains. The pottery is typical of the late Hellenistic era – say between the beginning of the second and the middle of the first centuries BC. This is a rather wide margin, and the coins enable us to bring it down to within narrower limits. But before we look at the coins associated with Qumran Ib, it will be helpful to offer a few general remarks about the role which coins play in the dating of all the periods of Qumran. A layer which contains a coin minted in, say, 100 BC cannot have ceased being occupied before that year (assuming that the coin was not dropped during a later period, a possibility which sometimes must be reckoned with!). However, the occupation in question may have begun earlier and ended later, or even begun later. Hence, one coin alone, or even a few coins from about the same time, cannot assist us very much in determining the span of a period of occupation. For this there has to be a sequence of coins. A layer yielding a sequence running without any lengthy break between, say, 100 and 50 BC can be said, roughly, to represent an occupation during that period; the fact that it does not yield samples from before 100 BC or after 50 BC is significant, and permits us to assume (as a rule) that no occupation took place beyond these dates.

Of course, there has to be a margin of error. Coins remain in circulation for some time, especially silver ones. Bronze coins, which are less durable, are rather more helpful since they tend to pass out of circulation more quickly. Another complication which may arise is the scarcity of a certain mintage due, perhaps, to political or economic factors. On the other hand, coin *hoards* are especially valuable, since they represent the varied coinage in circulation at a single time, namely the time at which the hoard was laid.

All of these considerations are pertinent at some stage or other in the interpretation of coin evidence at Qumran. In the case of period Ib, about 80% of the coins recovered have been identified, the remainder being illegible. The earliest coins are Seleucid, minted by the Hellenistic kings who either in fact or nominally ruled over Syria and Palestine during the second century BC. Once the independent Jewish rulers of the Hasmonaean dynasty began to mint their own coins, Seleucid coins were replaced. Six of the Seleucid coins are silver, and six bronze, which are more useful for dating, covering the period between 200 and 130 BC. Among Jewish coins, there are bronzes from the reigns of Aristobulus (104–103 BC; one coin), Alexander Jannaeus (103–76 BC; one hundred and forty-three); and several for later monarchs. There is one which de Vaux believed could be assigned to the reign of John Hyrcanus (135–104 BC), but in recent years it has come to be seriously doubted whether this monarch in fact minted coins at all. It is therefore safest to disregard this one specimen.

From this sequence, we can plausibly conclude that Qumran Ib began somewhere early in the first century BC or conceivably at the very end of the second. Irrespective of the number of coins minted by Alexander Jannaeus, it is surprising that more coins from the period before his reign are not represented, and the most likely reason for this is not that the men of

Qumran had an aversion to Seleucid coins, or went without money, but that there were many fewer of them – that is, we are into Qumran period Ia. For this period, it will be remembered, we have no dates; but the beginning of Ib coincided with the end of Ia, and the paucity of archaeological remains suggest that Ia was of rather short duration. The beginning of the community's existence at Qumran, therefore, belongs probably in the second half of the second century BC. As we shall see, a majority of scholars are inclined to believe, on the evidence of the scrolls, that the establishment of a community at Qumran took place close to 150 BC. It might as well be said that the archaeological evidence permits this date, but does not strongly support it.

The end of period Ib presents us with another kind of problem. There are clear signs of both a fire and an earthquake associated with the end of Ib, together with evidence that the site was then either totally or largely abandoned for a considerable time. But there is no way of telling for certain whether the fire preceded the earthquake, or vice versa, or whether the two were simultaneous. It could have been the fire, or the earthquake, or both, which brought about the abandonment of Qumran. De Vaux's theory is that the earthquake caused the fire and that the combination of both drove away the inhabitants. He defends this interpretation on the grounds that it is the most economical and that there is nothing to contradict it. Yet why these events should lead to the settlement being virtually deserted for a long time has puzzled some scholars, and with good reason. The damage caused, as far as can be seen, was not beyond fairly speedy repair. And since the inhabitants did not dwell in the settlement but in tents or caves, they could easily have continued to inhabit the vicinity while restoring the Qumran buildings.

Another explanation is that the fire was brought about by a military action which also drove the men of Qumran away. Since the likelihood of an earthquake coinciding with this attack is remote, this view assumes that the earthquake struck after Qumran had been deserted, and explains why the damage it caused was not repaired. Had the earthquake preceded the fire, on this view, the damage would have been put right. This is in some respects a rather more attractive suggestion than de Vaux's 'economical' one, but it is not without its own problems. Before we consider them any further, however, let us examine the archaeological evidence with which we are working.

The most striking clues are those pointing to the earthquake, and in particular the rift in the cistern to the east of the main block (Plate 9). The whole of the eastern edge of the Qumran outcrop in fact dropped by nearly two feet (see the line of the shift on Plan 3). From the reconstruction work

Plate 9   A view of the cistern to the east of the main block, looking
south. The cracked steps caused by the earthquake at the end
of Period Ib are the most dramatic evidence at Qumran of this
disaster.

which commenced period II we know also that there was damage to the tower (and perhaps also to part of the western wall, although we know that over the years the Qumran outcrop has actually been shrinking due to the crumbling away of the edges). Now, we are very probably able to date the earthquake which caused the damage at Qumran. The Jewish historian Josephus[1] records that one occurred in the seventh year of Herod the Great, namely 31 BC. We can say, then, that Qumran Ib ended either in 31 BC or before it.

Now for the fire, traces of which are widespread. There is an extensive layer of ash, mostly the remains of palm-thatch roofing, probably scattered by the wind since it lies both inside and well outside the buildings. Against the interpretation of de Vaux, some members of the team of excavators were inclined to believe that this conflagration could hardly have been caused by accident or by earthquake, but only by a deliberate and systematic burning such as might follow a successful military attack. But is such an attack likely to have taken place? The most plausible occasion for such hostility is some-where close to 40 BC, with an existing power struggle between the Hasmon-aean ruler Antigonus and Herod. Antigonus enlisted the support of the Parthians, whose powerful empire lay to the east; these were very happy indeed to accept the pretext to invade Palestine. Herod, on the other hand, was aided by the Romans. A good deal of the fighting between the two sides took place in the region of the Jordan valley and an attack from either side on Qumran is by no means out of the question. What the purpose or benefit of such an attack may have been is another question altogether. There is certainly no evidence that the invaders made use of the site despite its strategic value.

Whatever the reason for the abandonment of Qumran, the evidence is impressive; a thick layer of mud was found to overlie the ashes to a depth of as much as 30 inches in places. This was no doubt due to the overflowing or leaking of the water system, which cannot therefore have received any attention for many years. This mud was used to furnish foundations for the rebuilding of Qumran at the beginning of period II; but before this could be done, a large accumulation of debris needed to be cleared away, which was deposited mainly into a small ravine to the north of the outcrop. This debris not only provides further confirmation of the decay into which the buildings had fallen, but also helps to date the abandonment because of the coins which it contained. None of the coins in this hoard dates from the reign of Herod the Great, a fact which supports the view that period Ib came to an end before this ruler was able to mint his own coins. Yet some of Herod's coins *did* turn up within the settlement in circumstances which appeared to associate them with period Ib. De Vaux regarded these as having

QUMRAN PERIOD II

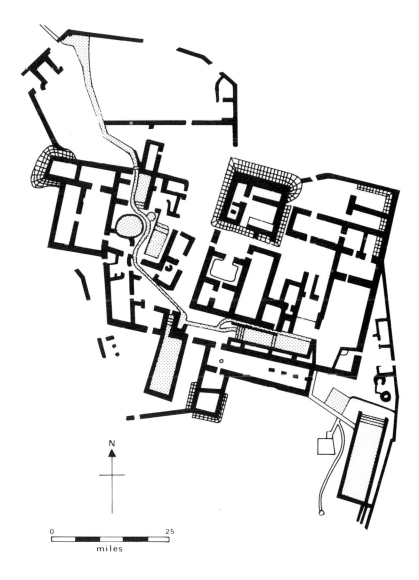

N

0   25
miles

Plan 4   Period II, *c.* 4 BC – 68 AD. The structures of Period Ib are
         retained, with buttressing in places; two reservoirs to the east of
         the main block are now unused.

been deposited not at the end of Ib but at the very beginning of II; that is, before the rebuilding had been carried out. Another view is that these coins betray a continued occupation of Qumran by a few inhabitants after the majority of the community had left. Again we see the complications which can arise in the interpretation of coin evidence.

Why the men of Qumran deserted their home for so long, where they went, and also why they returned when they did, are questions to which we can offer only speculations. There is no doubt (as we shall presently see) that it was the same community of period Ib which inhabited Qumran during period II. Since (as we shall also see) the beginning of period II seems to coincide more or less with the end of Herod's reign, it is tempting to conclude that the behaviour of the community was determined by the attitude and the actions of that king. But even this assumption can lead to opposing views; it has been maintained both that Herod showed favour to the community (and if the community were Essenes, as is likely, we have Josephus' testimony to this effect); but also that Herod persecuted them! As to where the community went, we have no idea whether they were temporarily assimilated into a wider movement with which they had affinities (such as the Essene movement, which appears to have been organised throughout Palestine, and perhaps even beyond), or whether they went as a group into exile somewhere. So far, there appears to be no trace at all of the Qumran community anywhere during this period.

Period II

In size, function and organisation, the community which occupied Qumran during this period is virtually identical with that of period Ib. Although a few alterations were carried out, the buildings were very substantially to the pattern of Ib. Some of the alterations involved strengthening areas of the settlement which had been damaged by the earthquake, especially in the north-west corner and the outer walls of the tower where buttressing was required. The major modifications can be identified by comparing the plan of period Ib (Plan 3) with that of II (Plan 4). As well as in a ravine to the north (already mentioned), debris was dumped outside the north and west walls. Among the rooms no longer used were the storage chambers in the ground floor of the tower, and the refectory annexe which was blocked off. The main extension was a store-room at the extreme north-east corner. The water system was also slightly modified, the large decantation reservoir in the north-west corner being left silted up, the cistern between the main block and the refectory divided into two, and the cisterns to the east of the main block – cracked by the earthquake – left unused by diverting the water channel directly into the south-east cistern. One result of all this reconstruction is that the use to which several of the rooms were put during period Ib is uncertain. But it seems likely, and we have assumed here, that as a rule the rooms at Qumran were restored in period II to their previous function.

In fixing the precise date of resettlement we have once again to utilise coin evidence, since as far as the pottery goes, the type is what is called 'Herodian'; and this has strong affinities with the pottery of Qumran Ib. Once again we find that with the coins problems of interpretation confront us. In this case the chief difficulty is with a hoard of coins consisting of 561 pieces of silver in three lots, all buried in pots below the level of period II. Two of these pots are of a type foreign to Qumran. Because of this fact, and because all of the hoard is, although below the level of period II, clearly *above* the level of period Ib, de Vaux takes the view that the hoard belongs to the period of rebuilding (period II) rather than destruction (period Ib). The majority of these coins are Tyrian currency which came into use in 126 BC and which, in fact, became the currency demanded by the temple authorities in Jerusalem for paying temple dues.[2] The most recent coin of this type in the hoard dates from the 118th year of Tyre, which is 9/8 BC, but we must bear in mind that a very small number of new Tyrian coins seems to have been minted until the 124th year of Tyre, the year 1 BC/AD. Since there are no coins as recent as this, it can be established that the hoard was most probably deposited between these two dates. But de Vaux has attempted a more precise definition of the date of commencement of period II using the coins discovered in the rubble cleared out from the ruins of Ib, to which we have already referred. This group of coins, it will be remembered, contained none from the reign of Herod, the majority forming a sequence which closes with the reign of Hyrcanus II (63 40 BC). One coin only falls outside this sequence, a coin which de Vaux ascribes to the reign of Herod Archelaus (4 BC–AD 6), and maintains that it came to be in the rubble with the other coins from period Ib because it was dropped during the work of clearing out Qumran at the beginning of period II. Hence, this coin can also assist us in establishing the date at which period II commenced. De Vaux's chain of reasoning is logical, if somewhat precarious. A majority of Qumran scholars have been inclined to accept the conclusion; and therefore it is widely agreed that Qumran period II commenced between 4 BC and 1 BC/AD.

The end of period II has been dated with even greater precision by de Vaux, and here too his deductions have been largely accepted. Again, it is a question of coin evidence and, again, the interpretation of this evidence warrants a question mark, even if in this instance a rather small one. The date arrived at for the end of period II, and thus the end of the community at Qumran, is AD 68; to be exact, the summer of that year. AD 68 was the third year of the war between the Jews and the Romans, the culmination of which was the destruction of the temple in AD 70, and its epilogue the capture of Masada in AD 74. Ever since the discovery during the excavations at Masada[3] of a scroll originating from Qumran, it has been suspected that the men of Qumran, or some of them, participated in the war against Rome. Such a theory takes account of the fact that period II at Qumran came to an end in conflagration, the result of an attack by Roman forces. Many of the rooms in the settlement, especially in the western block, were found to be full of debris from collapsed ceilings, and ash from burnt roofs lay everywhere. The most dramatic evidence of what transpired were Roman iron arrowheads which established that the occupants of Qumran had not simply deserted their home in the face of the legionaries, but had put up resistance. Those who did not remain had probably already deposited in one of the caves of the southern edge of the Qumran outcrop – now known as Cave 4 – what scrolls they were able to gather, having no time to store them properly or even arrange them neatly. Possibly they hoped to return after a short while to reclaim them.

It has also been suggested that Qumran was at this time occupied not by the Qumran community but by a group of Jewish warriors who expelled the inhabitants. These warriors, later driven from Qumran by Roman forces, withdrew to Masada, taking with them some manuscripts from the settlement, one of which has been found there. But it could as well have been taken by refugees from the community.

With the aid of Josephus' account of the events of the Jewish war, we can fit the capture of Qumran into the movements of Roman forces in the area. During the summer of AD 68 the legion X *Fretensis* – if we follow the generally accepted interpretation of Josephus at this point – was stationed at Jericho. It was during his stay here that the commander of the Roman forces fighting in Judaea, the future emperor Vespasian, conducted his famous (or notorious) experiment in which he tested the buoyancy of the Dead Sea by throwing captives with their hands tied behind their backs into the water. (The captives chosen were of course non-swimmers, but they all floated.)

Josephus does not mention any fighting in the immediate vicinity of Qumran, but a raid on Qumran – which, it will be remembered, occupied a very convenient strategic position – could have taken place during this period. The coin evidence, which yet again comes to the fore, accords perfectly with this possibility. During the war with Rome, the Jewish authorities minted their own coins, beginning with the first year of the war, proclaimed on the inscriptions as 'year 1 of the Liberation of Zion'. From

QUMRAN PERIOD III

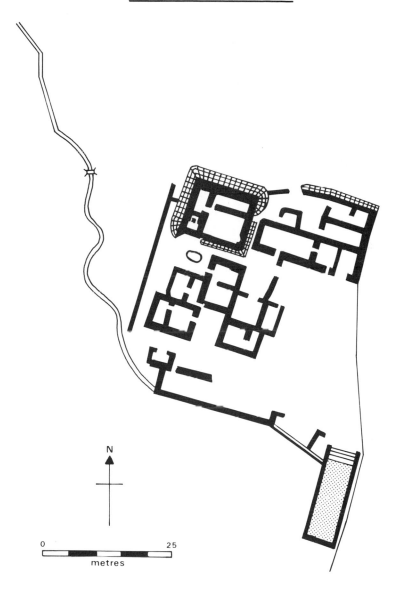

N

0   25
metres

Plan 5   Period III. The Roman occupation utilised only part of the main
block and one cistern in the south-east corner, served by a
simplified water-channel.

the second year of the war (67–8, the year being reckoned from the spring), 83 such coins were found at Qumran, but there were only 5 from the third year and none from the fourth or fifth years. The coins were found mostly in lots, one collection of 39 coins originally held in a bag and left just outside the western wall, and another in a decantation basin where together with other debris they had been cleared out at the beginning of period III. On the face of it, this is quite compelling evidence to confirm that Qumran period II came to an end early in the third year of the war, namely during the middle of 68 BC; and this conclusion is supported by the sequence of coins belonging to period III.

With the arrival of the Romans, the life of the community at Qumran ceased for good. What became of its members is another story; there is a body of opinion which holds that many of them were absorbed into the church with which the community had a number of beliefs and practices in common (in addition to several crucial differences). There is also the view that it retained its identity either in Palestine or elsewhere, since there are some striking similarities between the teachings of the community and those of a Babylonian Jewish group known as the Qara'ites, whom we hear of many centuries later. It is hard to believe that the community simply died out.

Period III

Immediately or shortly after the termination of Qumran period II, the Romans themselves occupied the site. Above the destruction layer, the coin sequence begins at AD 67/8, fairly exactly where the sequence of period II ends. Many of the coins associated with this period are of the mint which Roman soldiers would have been paid, struck at Caesarea. The neatness of the coin sequences is perhaps to an extent fortuitous; and some scholars would like to maintain that it is also misleading; for instance, the transition from Jewish to Roman coinage does not necessarily mean a change of occupation from Jews to Romans, but entails only a change in the accessibility of certain coinage at Qumran. Nor, in fact, does the presence of coins dating from AD 67/8 at the beginning of the period III sequence prove that the Roman occupation began at this juncture; one might indeed expect some coins from previous years which would still be in circulation. But on the other hand, soldiers were quite probably paid in newly-minted coins; and although the coin evidence is not as conclusive as it may appear, it is sufficiently impressive to require concrete evidence, rather than speculation, to undermine its testimony.

The rather limited rebuilding which characterises Qumran period III must therefore be attributed to a Roman garrison which was left here during the war (Plan 5). Only a part of the ruins was reoccupied, namely the main block (except for the south-eastern quarter). The tower and the north wall of this block were reinforced, and on all sides the occupied area was made more secure by digging a ditch along the western wall and closing entrances in the southern wall. Since the occupants of this fort were now fewer in number than during period II, less water was needed and hence only one of the cisterns remained in use, the largest one lying in the south-east corner. The water channel was simplified in order to bring the flow directly from the north-west corner, where it still entered the buildings, to the opposite corner, which also involved filling in the big south cistern and routing the channel over it; this remains something of a puzzle.

The facilities at Qumran during this period are rudimentary. One oven was built above the ruins at the foot of the tower. Very little pottery was preserved from this period, and the potter's workshop was in fact utilised as a lime-store. Generally, the occupation of this period has left few traces and was probably of short duration. After the end of Roman military operations in the area with the fall of Masada in AD 74, there would appear to have been very little need for Qumran to remain occupied. A fairly prompt departure is suggested by the coins remaining from this period. There is one coin from AD 87, but it was recovered outside the buildings and cannot definitely be connected with any occupation of Qumran. In fact, there is no coin issued in Palestine and represented at Qumran after the year 72/73 except this one. We can therefore conclude that the Romans left shortly after their successful capture of the fortress of Masada, the last remaining stronghold of the Jewish forces which held out long after the remainder of the country had been subjugated.

A further brief occupation of Qumran, during the second Jewish war of AD 132–5 should be recorded. This is betrayed only by the presence of Jewish coins minted during that war. Whether Jewish forces used the site as a military base or as a refuge during the concluding stages of the conflict we cannot tell for certain. We can say, however, that from their departure until the arrival of the archaeologists in the wake of the scrolls' discovery, Khirbet Qumran remained a well-known but little-considered ruin. Only the name Khirbet el-Yahud (Jews' ruin) by which it was also known, might have given a hint of what once had occurred on this unlikely spot.

The surrounding area

No account of Qumran can afford to ignore the fact that the settlement as a whole was an agricultural complex with a community centre as the focus of its life. Consequently, a brief description of the surrounding areas requires to be included in any survey. To begin with, beside the ruins of Qumran lies an impressive cemetery, beginning fifty yards to the east of the buildings and extending over the remainder of the outcrop and over four hillocks still further east. In all, over a thousand tombs have been counted, and the entire cemetery clearly divides into two sections. The larger of these, lying on the outcrop itself, contains graves which are arranged in neat rows separated by two alleys into three plots. Each of the graves in this section is marked by an oval-shaped heap of stones on the surface, and every grave except one is orientated in the unusual north-south axis. During the seasons of excavation, beginning with the preliminary and inconclusive survey of 1949, twenty-six of these graves, selected from different parts of this section of the cemetery, were investigated. In each case, the same method of interment was found; a rectangular cavity of between four and six feet deep had been dug, and a niche cut horizontally to accommodate the corpse. After burial the tomb was sealed. The corpse lay on its back with the head at the southern end. The significance of this is not at all clear, but it was observed that in the event of a resurrection being envisaged, the revived body would presumably be intended to face north. All the skeletons in this section of the cemetery were male.

In the other section, covering the hillocks beyond the outcrop and furthest from the buildings, the graves are not so tidily set out, nor is the orientation consistent. Of the six skeletons which were examined from here four were identified as female and one as that of a child. All of them had apparently died young and of unnatural causes. The difference between the two sections of this cemetery naturally raises questions about the composition of the community. It is virtually certain that the well-ordered section containing exclusively male skeletons was the resting place for the members of the community, which seems in this case to have comprised male members only. The pottery found in the graves was identical with that found in the buildings during their occupation by the community. However, the same can be said of pottery recovered from the other graves, which makes it virtually certain that these too were dug by members of the community. The bodies interred here, including those of women and children, are perhaps those of refugees or travellers. This assumes that the men of Qumran accepted outsiders into their midst. Could these women and children, have been the families of members of the community? The suggestion offered by de Vaux that some groups within the community *did* marry is supported by the contents of two other small cemeteries, one to the north of the Qumran outcrop and one just south of the Wadi Qumran. From the former of these, two graves were

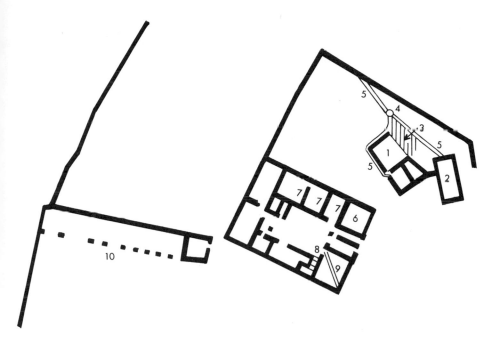

FESHKHA

1. Plastered basin

2. Basin

3. Paving

4. Tank

5. Channel

6. Store

7. Low dividing walls

8. Stairs to 1st floor

9. Drain

10. Pillars

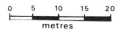

```
0    5   10   15   20
├──┼──┼──┼──┤
      metres
```

Plan 6   The Feshkha complex (see pp. 67–68). The main block comprises a courtyard with surrounding rooms. The system of channels and basins to the north remains something of a puzzle.

Plate 10　A general view of Feshkha during excavations, looking north-
east (compare plan 6).

excavated and yielded one male and one female skeleton; from the latter,
four graves yielded one female skeleton and those of three children. It seems
that we should assume, from the foregoing evidence at least, that although
the Qumran community was predominantly or even exclusively male, there
was a place within the settlement for women and children, either temporarily
or permanently, officially or unofficially.

From as early as the Israelite period at Qumran, a wall ran south from the
buildings which probably marked the boundary of a farming estate. During
periods I–II this wall reached as far south as ᶜAin Feshkha, where a section
of it remains, although the method of its construction is different from that
of its Qumran end. Just north of ᶜAin Feshkha are the remains of a small
building about forty feet square, divided into three rooms and standing close

to the boundary wall just mentioned. The very small amount of pottery recovered from it is contemporary with Qumran I–II, and the building seems to have served some purpose connected with the agricultural activities of the community. South of this building, the coastal plain is watered by numerous springs whose position is clearly visible from the Qumran outcrop as a wide patch of green in the otherwise brown landscape (Plate 10). The larger spring at Feshkha itself lies at the southern end of this territory, and it is here that a substantial structure was excavated in 1958, after having been investigated during the final season at Qumran. The few remains of the structure which were visible on the surface turned out to be those of a rectangular building 75 feet by 60 feet, comprising a central courtyard surrounded by rooms, and with a lean-to building on the south and an enclosure on the north (Plan 6 and Plate 21). From the pottery and the coins found here it emerged that this building was inhabited during periods I–II at Qumran, with three stages of occupation discernible. The first, Feshkha I, which has left little trace, probably corresponds to Qumran Ib; Feshkha II, which ended in a fire, to Qumran II; but Feshkha III contains coins of both the first and second centuries AD. It was certainly inhabited during the second Jewish war of 132–135, and perhaps earlier. In both cases occupation was confined to only part of the building and there is no correspondence with Qumran III.

The entire history of the Feshkha building closely matches that of Qumran periods I–III, and there is no reason to doubt that the installation here was an integral part of the Qumran complex. It is nonetheless worthwhile pointing out that there is at Feshkha no trace of the earthquake or of a fire such as were found to have taken place at the close of Qumran Ib, and there are no clues to tell us whether or not Feshkha was abandoned during the thirty years or so which passed between the end of Qumran Ib and the beginning of Qumran II.

The most fascinating of the Feshkah structures is a complex of channels north-east of the main building, dating from period II. Its function continues to puzzle and challenge the ingenuity of archaeologists and other scholars. De Vaux concluded after a good deal of cogitation that it most probably served as a tannery where leather was cured. Of all the guesses, this one remains perhaps the least improbable. Like all of the explanations offered, it is not without objections – of which de Vaux was himself well aware. But whatever the function of this part of the Feshkha installation, the whole structure was surely connected with the agricultural activity which was possible in this area, and which enabled the community of Qumran to achieve something close to economic self-sufficiency. The springs at Feshkha provided water for flocks and herds, and the reeds which grow beside them provided fodder. Fruit from date-palms which grew, perhaps quite abundantly, on the coastal plain in the vicinity of Feshkha was quite probably stored here to dry. Some industrial work may also have been carried on here; making matting from the reeds, working the timber from the palm-trees, and, as has been suggested, tanning.

The archaeological data presented above allow us to fix the dates during which Qumran was occupied, and show us also the kind of activities which could have taken place and did take place both in the settlement at Qumran and the surrounding region. In order to answer more fully the question, 'What was life like at Qumran?' we shall have to make use of the literary evidence, both from ancient authors who were acquainted with Qumran or its inhabitants, and from the Qumran scrolls themselves. With these resources, we can fill in many details of a picture of which, thanks to competent digging and scrupulous argumentation to interpret the evidence, we have achieved already more than a mere outline.

Notes

1. *Jewish Antiquities*, XV, 121–147; *Jewish War*, I, 370–380.
2. For the rabbinic evidence, see the Mishnah *Bekhoroth*, 8;7: Tosefta *Ketuboth*, 13;4. Only Roman coins were minted in Palestine in New Testament times; hence the need for temple money-changers (Mark 11:15).
3. See Y. Yadin, 'The Excavation of Masada,' *Israel Exploration Journal* 15 (1965), pp. 81–2; 105–8.

Bibliographical Note

The definitive account in English of the excavations at Qumran is the revised and translated text of de Vaux's Schweich Lectures of 1959, *Archaeology and the Dead Sea Scrolls*, Oxford, 1972. Reports of the excavations originally appeared at intervals in the *Revue Biblique* (in French). The report of Cross and Milik on the sites in the Buqei'a is available in English in *B.A.S.O.R.* 142 (1956), pp. 5–17. The excavations of P. Bar-Adon near ʿAin el-Ghuweir are described in 'Another Settlement of the Judean Desert', *B.A.S.O.R.* 227 (1977), pp. 1–25. As a pictorial guide to Qumran, J. M. Allegro, *The People of the Dead Sea Scrolls*, London, 1959, is recommended. The books by Cross and Milik mentioned in the bibliographical note to chapter 2 are informative also in respect of the archaeological data, and Milik in particular indicates areas of disagreement with de Vaux. E. W. G. Masterman's visits to the region are described in the *Palestine Exploration Fund Quarterly Statements* from 1902–13, and make fascinating reading.

4

The Inhabitants: Identification and Origins

Rarely in biblical archaeology do excavations of an ancient city proceed independently of literary data (which usually furnish a starting point for the archaeological work). In the case of Qumran, the connection of the ruins with the scrolls enabled the excavators to build their interpretation upon indications in the scrolls as to the manner of life of the community whose home was being investigated. For example, the very existence of the scrolls prompted the identification of the Qumran scriptorium, and the information that the men of Qumran practised frequent bathing explained the size and manner of construction of the elaborate water-system – a feature of the settlement which might otherwise have continued to puzzle us.

Before the digging at Qumran commenced, it was known that the scrolls were the product of a Jewish group different in many ways from the rest of the Judaism of its time, living a religious way of life as a community of exile. Such insight informed the approach towards the archaeological data, although it would be wrong to conclude that the role of archaeology turned out in this case to be no more than that of illustrating the literary evidence, because in fact the scrolls give us a very unbalanced picture of the everyday life of the community, concentrating on its beliefs, some of its practices and laws, and offering only elusive scraps of historical information. Very little of the economic working of the community is revealed, and some of the information which we are afforded is too fragmentary to be of use, or even quite contradictory. On the other hand, the results of the excavations tell us rather little about the beliefs or the religious practices of the men of Qumran. Hence the literary and archaeological data are very much complementary, and we must allow each to speak on matters where its information is likely to be reliable.

There is, besides, another source of literary information which must be acknowledged as of the utmost importance. Accounts from ancient authors at the time of the Qumran community speak of an order known as the 'Essenes' whose beliefs and practices corresponded remarkably with those revealed in the scrolls and also with certain data brought to light in the excavations. It was through such accounts, in fact, that scholars first became

Plate 11   A view towards the west across the western block, seen from
the tower. In the foreground, beyond the corridor, is the
ancient round cistern, with storerooms beyond. Behind these,
on the other side of the ravine, is the limestone terrace with the
Wadi Qumran on the left.

convinced that a connection existed between these ancient cave manuscripts and the nearby ruins, and pressed for a reopening of the question which the preliminary survey of Khirbet Qumran seemed to have closed.

The most important of the ancient reports, in this respect, occurs in the fifth book of the *Natural History* of the Roman traveller and statesman Pliny the elder. In the course of a description of Palestine he writes,

> On the western shore [of the Dead Sea] are settled the Essenes, some distance removed from the unhealthy odours of the shore itself. They are a lonely people, the most extraordinary in the world, living without women, without love and without money, having only the palm-trees for company. Yet they maintain their numbers, for recruits come to them in abundance, men weary of life or driven by changes of fortune to adopt their way of living. And thus through countless ages, incredible as it may seem, this people among whom no children are born has survived, so prolific for them is the repentance which others feel for their lives. Further down from these was the town of En-gedi, which in the fertility of its soil and palm-groves was second only to Jerusalem [possibly a mistake for 'Jericho'], but today is reduced, like it, to a heap of ashes. Then comes the fortress of Masada in the mountains . . .

This description obviously applies to the period after the first Jewish war, in which En-gedi, like Jerusalem (or Jericho) was 'destroyed' by the Romans. But by this time, as we have learnt, Qumran was either deserted or occupied by Roman soldiers. It may be that Pliny was drawing either on his own memory or on notes which referred to the situation prior to the Jewish war. Writing after these events, of which he had some knowledge, Pliny was yet unaware of that this settlement had been brought to an end. Most scholars have maintained that it is Qumran to which Pliny refers, and that the community of Qumran was therefore Essene. Certainly, no other site in this region corresponds anything like so well as Qumran to Pliny's portrait; it is some distance from the shore, it lies north of En-gedi (and Pliny was moving from north to south, as the mention of Masada after En-gedi makes clear); and date palms grew on the plain where the freshwater springs were located, between Qumran and Feshkha. The findings at the Qumran cemetery suggest, as we have seen, that the community was an all-male society, and further points of identity between Pliny's group and the men of Qumran will emerge presently.

Pliny's information, then, sets us off in search of a fuller description of his Essenes, and this we find in the writings of the Jewish historian Josephus, a contemporary of Pliny. In his *Jewish War*, written towards the end of the first century AD, Josephus describes three 'schools' of Judaism, presenting them rather like philosophical systems, and claiming a first-hand knowledge of each of them (a claim which, like much of what Josephus says, is quite probably exaggerated). One of these 'schools' is that of the Essenes, and Josephus writes far more about them than about the other two, the Pharisees and the Sadducees, put together. From this description and from other references in Josephus works, there emerges an order of men who have no city of their own but settle in existing cities. They are celibate, but there is a branch of the order which permits marriage. Their chief interest is in ancient writings and the healing properties of herbs and stones. They have no private wealth, but share all things in common. Josephus describes individual Essenes on a few occasions and in all but one case they utter predictions which are subsequently fulfilled.[1] The remaining case is an Essene military leader during the Jewish war,[2] and Josephus hints at a wider Essene involvement in this enterprise by referring to their undergoing torture at the hands of the Romans. The Romans do not appear to have practised indiscriminate persecution of Jews during the war, and it seems therefore that the Essenes were identified as one of the rebellious elements of the population, or at least produced from their numbers several individuals who played a prominent role in the revolt. This may help to explain the destruction of Qumran II.

Josephus also tells us of the manner of initiation into the Essenes, and this instance provides the most striking similarity between his Essenes and the men of Qumran, for the *Community Rule* (1QS) contains details of the stages of initiation at Qumran. Other correspondences between Josephus' description and the scrolls include the celebration of a sacred meal and the practice of frequent bathing.

Another account of the Essenes is furnished by the Jewish philosopher Philo of Alexandria, who lived during the first half of the first century AD. Philo informs us that the Essenes numbered 4,000, agreeing with Josephus that they lived in no one city of their own; indeed, according to Philo they avoided all cities and lived in villages. They also appear as lovers of peace and as expert agriculturalists, their chief occupations being listed as planters, sowers, herdsmen, beekeepers and craftsmen.

Allowing for a certain bias in each of these reports, there is a good deal of agreement between the two ancient authors and, as we have noted, with the scrolls. Perhaps the one major problem posed by both these descriptions is that they make no mention of Qumran. Yet both authors are drawing their knowledge from the period in which Qumran flourished. It is possible that Josephus was aware of the destruction of Qumran and therefore omitted to mention it, and that Philo was relying largely upon hearsay and was unaware of Qumran as an Essene centre of any special significance. Perhaps, if he knew of it, he regarded it as one of the 'villages'. But we should be wary of dismissing such problems too hastily. The Qumran scrolls themselves suggest the existence of other communities, which are called 'camps', and the relationship between these and Qumran is not at all easy to establish. For our purposes, the issue is how far we can use Josephus and Philo in reconstructing life in a settlement of which they do not seem to have heard. We are unwise to use their information unreservedly. Moreover, if the men at Qumran were Essenes – as the great majority of scholars take to be the case – they need not have been typical Essenes, if such existed. While we must draw on our ancient authors, therefore, we should do so with caution.

Even when we have at our disposal data from ancient authors, scrolls and archaeology, we find ourselves deprived of answers to many basic questions. Nowhere do we find any clear account of the origin of the Qumran community, or the Essenes, and we are obliged to interpret the usually cryptic allusions in the scrolls. Attention has been focused particularly on a set of commentaries on biblical books, chiefly Isaiah, Habakkuk, Nahum and Psalms, where the text is accompanied by an interpretation which applies it to events in the history of the community. But the events do not necessarily appear in chronological order, and many of the characters who seem to have played an important part in the history are designated by nicknames such as 'Wicked Priest', 'Man of the Lie', 'Spouter of Lies', 'Wrathful Lion-Cub', and so forth. Identifying these characters is a delicate matter; even if (as is usually assumed) these nicknames regularly apply to the same person, and that what is said of these persons is accurately remembered, we cannot be sure that we can identify them with known personalities from Jewish history. Many of the events in which they take part occurred within the community without repercussion in the outside world. In view of all this, it is extremely difficult to establish the circumstances in which the community at Qumran came into being. It is even more difficult to discover the prehistory of the community, and yet it is precisely in this period that we might expect to gain an understanding of the fundamental characteristics of Qumran belief and practice.

For the development of the community of Qumran, we are provided with a framework by the archaeological data, and we can hope to be able to correlate with these data aspects of the organisation and, to some extent, the beliefs of the community. But such a task entails a critical examination of the scrolls; and this is no easy task, since in its writings the community displays little awareness of or interest in its own evolution.

In tracing the origin of the community, we shall begin by recognising it as an Essene type. This in turn requires us to accept that other communities associated with and perhaps similar to that at Qumran also existed. The key questions then emerge as follows, what is the origin of the Essenes? what is the origin of the Essene settlement at Qumran? and what is the relationship between the Essene communities at Qumran and elsewhere?

These three questions are, of course, interrelated, and we can best begin to try and answer them by considering passages in the scrolls which are generally recognised as alluding to the period before the Essenes came to Qumran. The most important of these passages opens the *Damascus Rule*,

> . . . when they were unfaithful and forsook Him, He hid His face from Israel and His sanctuary and delivered them up to the sword. But remembering the Covenant of the forefathers, He left a remnant to Israel and did not deliver it up to be destroyed. And in the age of wrath, three hundred and ninety years after He had given them into the hand of king Nebuchadnezzar of Babylon, He visited them, and He caused a plant root to spring from Israel and Aaron to inherit His Land and to prosper on the good things of His earth. And they perceived their iniquity and recognised that they were guilty men, yet for twenty years they were like blind men groping for the way. And God observed their deeds . . . and He raised for them a Teacher of Righteousness to guide them in the way of His heart (CD I, 3–11; *D.S.S.E.* p. 97).[3]

The interpretation of this statement is a crucial matter, and we shall best proceed by dividing the early history of the Essenes into four stages – the remnant, the age of wrath, the twenty years, and the Teacher of Righteousness.

1. The remnant.   The origins of the Essenes are traced back to the survivors of the Babylonian exile which occurred in 58//6 BC. Elsewhere in the *Damascus Rule*[4] this remnant is the recipient of a new covenant, or a re-affirmation of the old covenant, under which God revealed to them 'the hidden things in which all Israel had gone astray.' In yet another passage[5] the remnant are called 'men of discernment' from Aaron and 'men of wisdom' from Israel, who 'dug a well'. This digging of a well is a well-known metaphor for establishing an interpretation of the law. It seems, therefore,

Figure 1 A table showing characteristic examples of pottery from
        Qumran and Feshkha. In particular, the types from Qumran Ib
        and Feshkha I may be compared. (The heavy lines represent
        actual fragments found, from which reconstruction of the entire
        vessel is achieved: dotted lines indicate probable rather than
        certain reconstruction.)

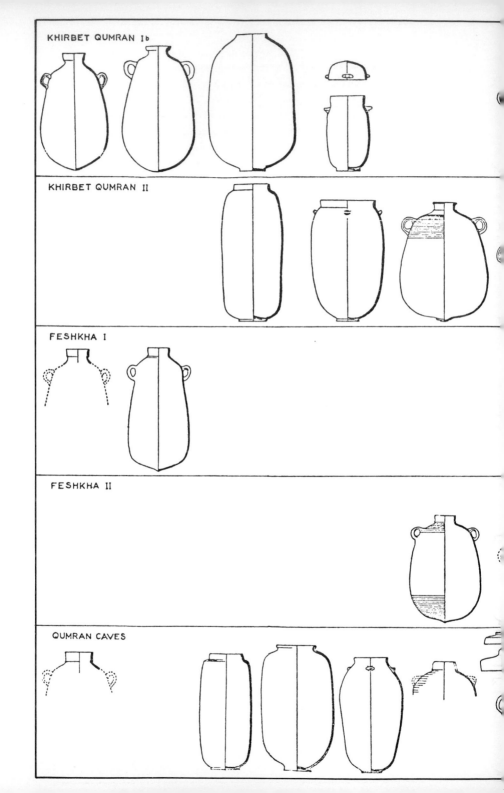

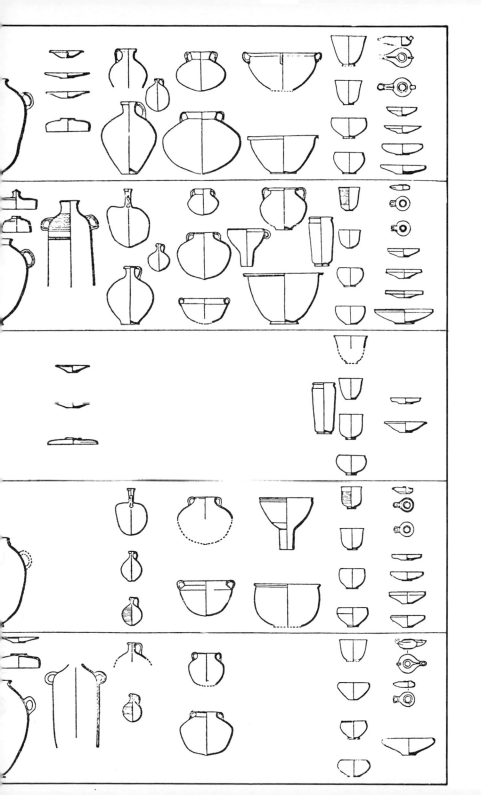

from all these passages that the Essenes regarded this post-exilic remnant as the germ of their own movement in three important respects; in having the covenant, in having the law and in having knowledge of the 'hidden things'. The 'hidden things', in fact, are defined in the *Damascus Rule* as pertaining to calendrical matters, the proper times of observance of sacred festivals. All of these features play an important role in distinguishing the Essenes from their fellow-Jews, and the Essenes' claim that the distinctive traits of Essenism go back almost as far as the exile needs to be taken very seriously.

2. The age of wrath.   This epoch is placed 390 years after the time when God delivered Israel to Nebuchadnezzar, namely 587/6 BC. Some scholars have suggested that the age of wrath is the exile itself, but the view generally held is that we should look to the early part of the second century BC for the beginning of this epoch. Although 390 years is derived from a prophecy of Ezekiel (4:5), it was probably chosen because it corresponded to the actual period of time involved, as the Essenes calculated it.

During these 390 years, the Jewish exile in Babylon had been formally ended by the edict of Cyrus and the Jews permitted to leave for their own land. A minority of them did return and Judaea became a province within the Persian empire, effectively governed by the High Priest, an office filled by the descendants of Zadok, the High Priest under Solomon. The temple at Jerusalem was rebuilt and the city became the centre of a religious community, a nation but not a state. This situation was little affected by the career of Alexander the Great, and when he died in 323 BC, his empire being divided eventually into smaller kingdoms, the Jews lived under the Ptolemies who ruled in Egypt and enjoyed much the same degree of religious autonomy as under the Persians. But with the irresistible tidal-wave of Hellenism which built up after the conquests of Alexander and the consolidation of Hellenistic kingdoms in the territory of the former Persian empire, the Jews were unable to preserve their way of life from the encroachments of a powerful and alluring cultural force. The dawn of the second century BC saw Palestine pass from Ptolemaic to Seleucid control, centred in Syria, and the change of allegiance accelerated tensions which had already become evident within the priestly and aristocratic ruling classes. A power-struggle among leading families in Jerusalem developed, in which the office of High Priest became a pawn, and Hellenisation of Jewish life and institutions the currency in which the favour of the Seleucid monarch could be bought. The early decades of the century saw the High Priesthood auctioned, during the course of which an illegally deposed and widely revered High Priest was assassinated. The occupation of the office was also transferred from the family of

Zadok.

These developments both partly took place but also came to a head in the reign of Antiochus IV, known as Epiphanes, who came to the Seleucid throne in 175. He had ambitions of an empire which were frustrated by the Romans, and was an especially keen promoter of Hellenistic culture, eager to respond to offers from Jerusalem to establish in the city a Greek *polis*, a society devoted to the Greek way of life, open only to 'citizens' drawn from the upper classes. The popular revolt which the king's enactments provoked led to his proscribing the practice of Judaism, pulling down the altar in the temple and replacing it with a shrine to Olympian Zeus, an object which the book of Daniel denounces as an 'abomination of desolation'. For three years a vigorous resistance was conducted under the leadership of Judas Maccabaeus which succeeded (in 164) in restoring the Jewish altar, rededicating the temple and forcing the revocation of proscription. One year later Antiochus died.

These events would aptly characterise an 'age of wrath' and their beginning could be dated with startling accuracy to very nearly 390 years after the capture of Jerusalem by Nebuchadnezzar.

During this 'age of wrath', we are told, a 'plant root' sprouted from Israel and from Aaron (that is, from laity and priests) to 'inherit His Land'. If 'Israel and Aaron' is a designation of the remnant to which we have previously referred, we are dealing with a splinter group; where did this splintering take place, and why? There are, broadly, two theories about this. One suggests that a group of loyal Jews developed in Palestine in opposition to the Hellenisation they were witnessing, and, taking the name of *Hasidim* ('Pious') they joined forces with Judas Maccabaeus against the Seleucids and the Hellenising Jews, as 1 Maccabees 2:42 describes. The other view is that the 'plant root' was a group of Babylonian Jews who migrated to Palestine, thus breaking away from an indigenous Babylonian Jewish group which regarded itself as the remnant.

The former view has always predominated and is represented in nearly all of the major books on Qumran or Essene history. The second, which is associated especially with the work of one scholar, Jerome Murphy-O'Connor, is gaining some ground. In either case, it seems that we ought to regard the movement from which the Qumran community sprang as having already a considerable history behind it.

3. The twenty years.   After the restoration of the temple and of Jewish practices, there was a period in which the authority of the Seleucid kings was weakened because of struggles for the throne. The needs of each claimant for the support of the Jews were exploited by Judas' successors, his brothers

Jonathan and Simon. Jonathan was an astute general and diplomat who manipulated events in order to consolidate his authority both constitutionally and in reality. In 152 he was offered the High Priesthood by the Seleucid king, and accepted this office, which carried with it political as well as religious rule over the Jews. Those who had supported the Maccabaean cause from a sense of outrage at the debasement of the High Priestly office were now faced with the assumption of that office by a Maccabaean leader who had no right to it, since he was not descended from Zadok – and indeed, he had accepted it as a gift from the Seleucid king, who had no right to bestow it!

The twenty years which are described as a time of groping and uncertainty by the 'plant root' could well correspond to the period between its emergence or arrival in Palestine and the crisis which Jonathan provoked. This identification is strengthened if we can identify Jonathan with a character known in the Qumran commentaries as the 'Wicked Priest', a contemporary of the 'Teacher of Righteousness' who arose after the 'twenty years' to guide those who were 'groping for the way'. The assumption that the Wicked Priest held the office of High Priest in Israel makes this figure the key to dating the Teacher and thus the establishment of the Qumran community.

4. The Teacher of Righteousness.   It is probable that we do not know the identity of this important person from accounts other than the Dead Sea scrolls. It has been speculated that he was the High Priest of Israel whom Jonathan ousted, but because he may have been regarded as High Priest by the Qumran community does not mean that he was so regarded by other Jews. We can be sure, however, that the Teacher was responsible for founding a community and bringing it to live at Qumran. Our knowledge of what transpired is confined to the allusions in the biblical commentaries, which suggest that he met severe opposition from within his own group and probably also from outside. He was apparently exiled for a time, and separated from his community. The teaching of this spiritual leader and the character and ideals of his community will be considered in the next chapter when we discuss the Qumran community during period Ia. But there is one remaining question; what became of the remainder of the group from which the Teacher and his community departed? Again, there are two main viewpoints. One of these, identifying the larger group with the Hasidim, supposes that the Teacher's group became the Essenes, and the remainder emerged as the Pharisees. The chief problem with this is in accounting for non-Qumran Essenes. The other view is that the wider group split into Qumran and non-Qumran Essenes. Although this split would have taken place in an atmosphere of hostility, it cannot be ruled out that the two forms of Essenism

later achieved a reconciliation.

A final word of warning, however. There is a flaw in this reconstruction, namely the 390 years. The fact is that ancient Jewish calculation of the post-exilic period was far from accurate. For the 410 years between the exile and Maccabaean revolt the book of Daniel gives nearly 490 years (ch. 9). There are further difficulties with the reconstruction, but for the present it remains, rightly, the major working hypothesis as to the formation of the community.

Notes

1. See *Antiquities* XV,373–79; *War* I,78–80.II,111
2. See *War*, II,567.III,11
3. References are to G. Vermes, *The Dead Sea Scrolls in English*, Penguin, 1975, quoted with permission of the publishers.
4. CD III,13f.
5. CD VI,2ff.

Bibliographical Note

The accounts of Pliny, Philo and Josephus are to be found in the following works, all available in English translation in the *Loeb Classical Library*, except for Philo's *Hypothetica*: Philo, *Quod Omnis Probus Liber Sit* (Every Good Man is Free) 12–13 (75–91), *Hypothetica* 11, 1–18 (as preserved in Eusebius, *Praeparatio Evangelica*); Josephus, *Life* 2 (10–12), *Jewish War* II, 119–161, *Jewish Antiquities* XVIII, 11–22; Pliny, *Natural History*, V, 17.

Other accounts of the Essenes in ancient writers are: Dio Chrysostom, preserved in Synesius, *Dio Chrysostom*, V (also in *Loeb*, p. 379), Hippolytus, *Refutatio Omnium Heresium* (Refutation of all Heresies) IX, 13–23 (probably based on Josephus, with some additional information of dubious value).

The texts of Josephus and Philo are reproduced, with comments, in M. Black, *The Scrolls and Christian Origins*, London, 1961, pp. 173–186.

On the origin of the Essenes, most of the standard works already introduced advocate an origin from the Hasidim (Cross, *The Ancient Library of Qumran*, pp. 98ff., Vermes, *The Dead Sea Scrolls*, pp. 142ff., Milik, *Ten Years of Discovery in the Judaean Wilderness*, p. 58). The theory of Babylonian origins is presented by J. Murphy-O'Connor in 'The Essenes and Their History', *Revue Biblique* 81 (1974), pp. 215–244, and a shorter statement is contained in 'The Essenes in Palestine', *Biblical Archaeologist* 40 (no. 3), 1977, pp. 100–124.

The most recent discussion of the Essenes, with extensive bibliographical information, is available in Schürer-Vermes-Millar, *The History of the Jewish People in the Age of Jesus Christ*, Edinburgh, 1979, II, pp. 555–590.

5

Qumran under the Teacher: Period Ia

If we know virtually nothing about the identity of the Teacher of Righteousness, we are able to learn a good deal about his character and his ideals, and thus about the community which he founded and led during its first years of life at Qumran. The scroll of *Hymns* from Cave 1 (1QH) is believed to contain several compositions of the Teacher himself; such hymns contain a fairly small number of recurring themes, couched in a vocabulary and idiom which is distinctive. The author thanks God for the grace and the strength which he has received, although he confesses to being undeserving of them since he is a worthless creature. He has suffered many persecutions at the hands of others and gives vent to his sorrow: especially grievous to him has been his betrayal and vilification by members within his own group. Yet such trials have served to sustain him, for God has made him into a rock on which his adversaries will shatter. He himself has become the standard by which the righteous and the wicked are distinguished.

The Teacher shows himself passionately devoted to the community which he has founded, and God has made him a father to them. He also uses a dramatic maternal image in speaking, with language reminiscent of messianic descriptions, of bringing forth the community as a woman giving birth, with all the attendant pains of parturition. This community/child, cleansed and purified by God, is an eternal assembly living in communion with the angels, a witness to the coming judgement of God and a bastion against the terrors of hell. They alone know the divine mysteries which God has revealed through the Teacher to them.

These hymns provide a clear impression of the eschatological intensity and the conviction of mission which the Teacher felt so deeply. He must also have been able to convey this to his disciples, who faithfully preserved not only his words, but also, substantially, his ideals. In reading these words it is certainly not difficult to be gripped by the force of personality which their author exerted. He was doubtless a man of intense piety and of humility and submission before God, yet one suspects that he was also authoritarian, even arrogant in his dealings with men.

The first members of the community at Qumran lived under a régime which combined attitudes and practices traditional within the group from which they came with novel elements deriving from the Teacher himself. It is far from easy always to distinguish the two. It appears that both the Teacher and his followers believed themselves to be the true representatives of the group from which they derived, and referred often in their legislation to the 'former ordinances', that is, the rules by which they had been governed prior to their life at Qumran. Although many scholars would disagree, it is probable that the fundamental issues on which the men at Qumran differed from their fellow-Jews were characteristic of the movement before part of it followed the Teacher to Qumran.

The move by some Essenes physically to separate themselves from the rest of Judaism was in all probability symptomatic of a breach which already existed. For the Essenes observed a different calendar from that followed by the rest of the nation, and any student of ancient Judaism will appreciate the enormity of that difference; calendrical observance was one of the criteria by which the rabbis later defined heresy. All Jews, and the Essenes especially, regarded the calendar as divinely ordained, as old as creation if not older. Times and seasons were an indispensable part of the order of all things, and in particular the sacred times such as sabbaths, new moons, annual festivals and new years. The heavenly bodies existed, it was believed, mainly in order to regulate times and seasons. With the Essenes, belief in the harmony of the heavenly bodies with that of the life of man extended to astrology: we have from the Qumran caves fragments of horoscopes to prove this.

The Essene calendar was based on the solar year. How this came about we are not certain; perhaps this solar calendar was once the calendar of all Israel. It is a calendar reflected not only in the Dead Sea scrolls but in other works such as the Book of Enoch and the Book of Jubilees – both of them known and copied at Qumran. According to this system, the year consisted of 364 days, made up of 52 weeks exactly, and twelve months of 30 days each with an extra day separating each 'quarter' of three months. There was also another way in which this solar year was divided, namely into seven periods of fifty days each, which were separated by festivals. Thanks to the *Temple Scroll*, we now know the names of some of the feasts which the Essenes apparently did not share with non-Essenes. The cycle commenced with Passover on the 14th day of the first month, Nisan. The feast of barley followed on the 26th of the same month. Fifty days later came Pentecost or Weeks, the festival of wheat and also the occasion for covenant renewal. After another fifty days came the festival of wine (on the 3rd day of the fifth month) and another fifty days culminated in the festival of oil. This was immediately followed by a festival of wood. On the 1st day of the seventh

Plate 12   Some of the curious deposits of animal bones found buried
within the settlement; in this case, beyond the northern wall
of the western block, close to the decantation reservoir.

month New Year was celebrated (in both the Essene and non-Essene Jewish
calendar there are two 'New Years', in spring and autumn); this autumnal
New Year was followed by the Day of Atonement and the feast of Taber-
nacles (Booths).

In addition to these festivals, the first day of each 'quarter' was celebrated,
as well as the first day of each month. Every seven years constituted a 'week
of years' and the seventh year of the 'week' was a sabbatical year. Every
seventh (sabbatical) year was a jubilee year. In the Book of Jubilees, history
is reckoned, as the title reveals, in periods of fifty years, or 'jubilees'.

The *Temple Scroll* presents the Essene festivals described above as being
observed in the future temple of Israel, whose cult was to be regulated
according to Essene rules. The Essenes of Qumran were well aware of the
difficulty which revising the existing calendar would create; under the system
currently in force 24 courses of priests served in rotation for a period of one

Plate 13   A deposit of animal bones overlaid with sherds.

week at a time, twice during the year. Since the Essene year contained not 48 but 52 weeks, it could not accommodate the established number of priestly courses. In fragments from Cave 4, therefore, we find a calculation by which the 24 courses and the 52 weeks were synchronised over a six-year period, each course serving 13 times instead of 12.

From parts of the *War Scroll* and now the *Temple Scroll*, it is clear that we err if we think of the men of Qumran as having simply withdrawn from Jewish society in expectation of an imminent divine intervention which would vindicate them as the true Israel over against not only the Gentiles but also the remainder of Israel. While there are texts which illustrate this kind of belief, others demonstrate clearly that the Qumran Essenes hoped for a future restoration of all Israel according to the Essene law. At the time of the Teacher, however, the Essenes regarded the rest of Israel as in flagrant breach of the divinely ordained laws about 'times and seasons', observing festivals at the wrong dates, which invalidated the whole cult. It is a moot point whether the Essenes differed so far as to calculate the beginning of the day from sunrise rather than sunset (as other Jews): it seems that at any rate the Sabbath was reckoned from sunset at Qumran as elsewhere.

Before passing to the next major difference between Essenes and non-Essenes, it is worth noticing the agricultural emphasis of the Essenes' annual festivals. This emphasis is not simply a direct result of the manner of life practised at Qumran, but surely has its roots in the pre-Qumran origins of the Essenes. It was pointed out by Philo that agriculture was characteristic of the lifestyle of all Essenes, perhaps connected with the dislike of cities which Philo also attributes to them. It is tempting to suggest that the Essene ideology may have a distinct socio-economic (i.e. agrarian) as much as a doctrinal basis – if, indeed, such factors can ever be wholly distinguished in any religious movement within Judaism or elsewhere.

The second major respect in which the Essenes diverged from their fellow-Jews was in refusing to participate in the temple cult. Josephus tells us that the Essenes of which he knows – which, we must remember, do not necessarily include the Qumran group – participated only to the extent of sending first-fruit offerings. The Essenes would have presumably made these offerings at the times dictated by their own calendar – and, as we have seen, the cultic calendar according to the *Temple Scroll* included more first-fruit festivals than we know of from the Old Testament. But while there are some Qumran texts which appear to legislate for participation in certain other temple activities, we can be virtually certain that the Essenes of Qumran did not involve themselves at all in the cult at Jerusalem; and probably neither did their fellow Essenes.

Rejection of the temple entailed rejection of sacrifice, since the Mosaic law prohibited sacrifice outside the one chosen sanctuary – which meant, for Essenes and non-Essenes alike, Jerusalem. It is hardly credible that sacrifices were offered at Qumran, although a curious discovery during the excavations raised the possibility. Several deposits of bare animal bones were uncovered, having been buried just below the ground between large sherds or in jars (Plates 12, 13): these were located in open spaces throughout the settlement, and belong mostly to period Ib. Some of the bones, which in no case could be reconstructed into whole skeletons, were identified as those of sheep, goats, lambs, kids, cows and oxen. The bones were charred and almost certainly the remains of cooked meals rather than sacrifices. Why were they buried? A likely answer is that the meals at which these animals were consumed had a sacred character such as required the bones to be treated in this particular way. Other, less plausible, solutions have been offered; certainly neither the scrolls nor the archaeological remains have provided any certain evidence that sacrifices were performed at Qumran.

Quite the contrary, in fact. In what may have been a primitive 'manifesto' of the early community, we read,

> They shall atone for sin by the practice of justice and by suffering the sorrows of affliction (1QS 8,3–4; *D.S.S.E.*, p. 85).
> They shall atone for guilty rebellion and for sins of unfaithfulness that they may obtain lovingkindness for the Land without the flesh of holocausts and the fat of sacrifice. And prayer rightly offered shall be as an acceptable fragrance of righteousness and perfection of way as a delectable freewill offering (1QS 9,4–5; *D.S.S.E.*, p. 87).

It was by the discipline of their life at Qumran that the community achieved what for other Jews was achieved through the temple cult. Indeed, the community thought of itself as a temple,

> (God) has commanded that a Sanctuary of men be built for Himself, that there they may send up, like the smoke of incense, the works of the Law (4QF1 1,6–7; *D.S.S.E.*, p. 246).

The buildings at Qumran, then, housed a temple, composed of men who offered their own existence as a sacrifice. We cannot fail to be reminded of the words of Paul in Romans 12:1,

> I implore you, then, brethren, by the mercies of God, to present your bodies a living sacrifice, holy, acceptable to God, a spiritual form of worship.

But we must not draw comparisons too closely. The men of Qumran had not abandoned cultic religion. Their substitution of a holy way of life devoted to the law for the sacrifices of the temple was a temporary measure only, and they had elaborate plans for the construction and liturgy of the temple which one day would stand in Jerusalem. In both this respect, and their devout attitude to the law of Moses, they stood apart from the Christians. As has already been remarked, it is misleading simply to describe the Qumran Essenes as having permanently 'dropped out' of Jewish society and adopted a new basis of religion. It may be that the earliest members of the community understood their task to win atonement for the Land (as in the text quoted above) as a necessary preparation for the restoration of the true Israel, with the focus of its life in the new, legitimate temple.

We come now to the third respect in which the Essenes differed from their fellow-Jews; interpretation of the Law. It is difficult to be precise about the extent of the differences, since we know far too little about how the Law was then interpreted outside Qumran. But we can see from the *Damascus*

Rule, for instance, that the Essenes were more strict than their contemporaries in forbidding remarriage and marriage between uncle and niece, as well as in what they permitted to be done on the Sabbath.

All in all, these three major areas of difference between Essenes and other Jews are rather too deep-seated to have come about merely as the result of a physical and spiritual retreat from Jerusalem on the part of some disgruntled and ultra-orthodox Jews during the middle of the second century BC. The move to Qumran should probably be seen as the outcome of these basic differences rather than the reason for them. They are, in all probability, distinctive features of Essenism which were brought to Qumran. Here they acquired new dimensions of meaning. In the first place, the region to which these Essenes retreated took on a symbolic quality. The same early 'manifesto' from which we have already quoted reads,

> . . . they shall separate from the habitation of ungodly men and shall go into the wilderness to prepare the way of Him; as it is written, *Prepare in the wilderness the way of . . . make straight in the desert a path for our God* (Isaiah 40:3) (1QS 8,13–14; *D.S.S.E.*, pp. 85–6).

This famous text – with which the gospel of Mark opens – was interpreted in a literal sense by the men of Qumran. The Hebrew word translated 'desert' is not the usual term but designates a particular area, namely the vicinity of the Dead Sea – the 'Arabah'. The prophecy had also a typological significance, however. It had once been uttered to the Jews in Babylon as a proclamation of the coming end of their exile and return to the Promised Land. To those at Qumran, it seemed that the land had never really been recovered; it was still not truly Israel's, and hence they saw themselves as preparing for that great event which still lay ahead. The 'path' they interpreted as the study of the Law, one of the most vital activities of the community at all periods of its life and one which took its place alongside the 'practice of justice' and 'suffering the sorrows of affliction' by which they 'atoned for the Land'. A vivid reminder of their predicament lay across the Dead Sea. Among the mountains beyond its eastern shore, almost opposite Qumran, stood the legendary Mount Nebo from which Moses had surveyed the Promised Land, a land to which the great lawgiver had brought the wandering Israelites but which he was not to reach.

If the geographical location of Qumran was full of significance, the site of the settlement itself also provided a source of imagery. The 'sorrows of affliction' of these Essenes included not only the loneliness of exile but the hardships of the unpleasant region to which they had retreated. Yet to a certain kind of mentality, such affliction can be a source of spiritual comfort. There is a remarkable passage in one of the hymns written by the Teacher

Plate 14   From the foot of the cliffs, a view east across the Qumran
outcrop to the Dead Sea. The remains of the aqueduct and,
beside it, of the ancient path from the cliffs and the Buqeiʿa
beyond, are in the foreground.

where, amid a confusion of images typical of his poetry, he perhaps offers
us a view of his place of retreat,

. . . Thou hast placed me beside a fountain of streams in an arid land,
and close to a spring of waters in a dry land, and beside a watered garden
[in a wilderness. For Thou didst set]* a plantation of cypress, pine and
cedar for Thy glory, trees of life beside a mysterious fountain hidden
among the trees by the water, and they put out a shoot of the everlasting
Plant. But before they did so, they took root and sent out their roots to
the watercourse that its stem might be open to the living waters and be
one with the everlasting spring (1QH 8,4–8; *D.S.S.E.* p. 176).

89

At other places we come across images of building,

> I shall be as one who enters a fortified city, as one who seeks a refuge behind a high wall . . . For Thou wilt set the foundation on rock and the framework by the measuring-cord of justice; and the tried stone [Thou wilt lay] by the plumb-line [of truth], to [build] a mighty [wall] which shall not sway; and no man entering there shall stagger (1QH 6,24–27; *D.S.S.E.* p. 171).

Perhaps even more striking is the following passage,

> By my hand Thou hast opened for them a well-spring and ditches . . . When I lift my hand to dig its ditches its roots shall cut deep into hardest rock . . . (1QH 8,21–23; *D.S.S.E.* pp. 177–178).

It requires little imagination to read these lines as reflections upon or even poetic descriptions of the newly-rebuilt settlement beside the Wadi Qumran, and a little north of the Feshkha oasis.

The Teacher and his community were not left in peace at Qumran. There is one incident in particular which the *Habakkuk Commentary* describes. The Wicked Priest

> purused the Teacher of Righteousness to the house of his exile that he might confuse him with his venomous fury. And at the time appointed for rest, for the Day of Atonement, he appeared before them to confuse them, and to cause them to stumble on the Day of Fasting, their Sabbath of repose (1QpHab 11,5–8; *D.S.S.E.* pp.241–242).

We are given very little idea of exactly what transpired or why. But it seems probable that, despite what nearly all commentators have assumed, the Teacher was not present at Qumran when the Wicked Priest made his visit. Although the 'house of his exile' could refer to Qumran, we learn from the Teacher's own hymns that he was exiled from his companions,

> They have banished me from my land like a bird from its nest; all my friends and brethren are driven far from me and hold me for a broken vessel (1QH 4,8–9; *D.S.S.E.* p. 161).

The Teacher also speaks in his hymns about being abandoned and despised by all the members of his community. Perhaps these bitter passages allude to a period of exile from Qumran. Yet finally, it seems, the Teacher and his group were reconciled, and, as the *Habakkuk Commentary* reports, the Wicked Priest was delivered into the hands of his enemies for what he had done to the Teacher and to the 'men of his council'.

We have a few allusions to specific events during period Ia which allow us to recognise that the founding of the community at Qumran was not achieved without opposition. If we are disappointed by the vagueness of the evidence, we need to realise that events involving the Teacher and his opponents are about the only clues we have to events which took place at any time within the history of the community.

What, then, can we say about the organisation of the early Qumran community? The *Community Rule*, which contains most of the relevant information, includes material from probably every period, and interpreting the historical sequence of the various rules and forms of organisation is a delicate and uncertain task. But the following description may well apply to period Ia. The leader of the community was called the Maskil (presumably at first the Teacher himself?) who understood the teaching of the Law and had 'true knowledge'. He was charged with assessing the character of all who wished to join the community, and with admitting or rejecting them. Once they were accepted the Maskil retained responsibility for their progress. As well as giving instruction he led the worship.

'Maskil' means 'wise', 'discerning', and was already used in the book of Daniel as a description of enlightened spiritual leaders (see Daniel 12:3). Matters of 'property' and 'justice' were under the jurisdiction of priests (of whom the Maskil was almost certainly one). We have perhaps only two examples of the rules of this early community. One regulation states simply that whoever 'turns aside from all that is commanded' on any point whatsoever is debarred from table fellowship and from the 'counsel' of the 'men of holiness'; this ban is effective until his deeds are again deemed worthy of readmission. Such a simple and undifferentiated rule best fits an early stage in the evolution of Qumran legislation; here all offences come under the same category, and one punishment alone is prescribed, a fairly lenient one which assumes that the culprit wishes to remain a member of the community and will mend his ways. From this rule we can also learn that the two most vital institutions of the community were the common meal and the 'counsel'; we shall have more to say of these in due course. Non-participation in both, however, amounted to exclusion from the 'living temple' of the community, deprived of both its fellowship and its wisdom.

A second rule from this period already contains an elaboration of the first one. It requires expulsion for anyone who deliberately infringes the law of Moses; no 'man of holiness' may associate with the culprit either in 'property' or in 'counsel'. Inadvertent misdemeanours, however, incurred only exclusion from the meal and the 'counsel'. A supplement to this rule interprets it to mean that in the second case the offender should not be asked his counsel nor participate in giving judgement for two years. If he reforms, he may nevertheless return to the 'court of inquiry' and the 'council', in accordance with the judgement of the congregation. Readmission is granted on condition that he commits no further inadvertent sin within two years. There follows a further qualification: for a single inadvertent sin, the offender does penance for two years, but for a deliberate sin the punishment is expulsion.

The present form of the rule betrays a process of development in which both offences and punishments are subjected to refinements and distinctions, a condition which probably responds to the widening experience of the community in administering disciplinary measures. An awareness of the need in some cases to expel a member of the community represents a stage in the process of compromise between idea and reality. Unadulterated 'spirit' cannot long survive without some degree of 'letter'.

There is, unfortunately, nothing that we can say about the economic life of this early community. We can be sure that it did not devote its time exclusively to religious rituals or study of the Law. Whatever precisely its members were expecting, they probably did not anticipate that their residence at Qumran would be lengthy. Adjustment in such circumstances to the requirements of a permanent settlement would be only partial.

Bibliographical Note

There is a brief discussion and an excellent bibliography in Vermes, *The Dead Sea Scrolls*, pp. 137–162. In this and the next chapter the following studies of the *Community Rule* have been closely followed: J. Murphy-O'-Connor, 'La Génèse Littéraire de la *Règle de la Communauté*', *Revue Biblique* 76 (1969) pp. 528–549; and J. Pouilly, *La Règle de la Communauté*, Gabalda, Paris, 1976.

* Brackets [ ] indicate words restored where there are gaps in the manuscripts.

6

Qumran in its Heyday: Period Ib

We have already seen that period Ib was ushered in by a substantial enlarge-
ment of the settlement necessitated by an increase in numbers. We shall see
presently how the way of life at Qumran changed as a result: but first let us
ask what caused the influx of new members, and what sort of men they may
have been. We may rule out any large-scale religious conversion or change
in fashion which brought a life of loneliness and hardship and strict discipline
into vogue. The answer must rather lie in developments within Jewish
society outside Qumran which prompted some to escape to a place of relative
security.

A widely-held opinion, which follows this line of reasoning, holds that
such refugees were Pharisees. According to Josephus, John Hyrcanus, ruler
and High Priest from 134–104 BC, fell out with the Pharisees, apparently
because of their opposition to his tenure of the High Priestly office. As a
result of his displeasure, many Pharisees may have been driven to seek
refuge at Qumran. Whether by so doing they would have placed themselves
out of his effective reach is doubtful, for the ruler had a fortress, called
Hyrcanion, only eight miles from Qumran and within easy reach across the
Buqeiʿa. But at Qumran the refugees might be considered to have put
themselves outside the orbit of Jewish society and therefore to be of no
further threat to Hyrcanus. The quarrel, as described by Josephus, coincided
with the beginning of period Ib at Qumran, and the view that the Essenes
and the Pharisees were descendants of the same religious group allows that
Qumran would have been a plausible refuge.

This theory is certainly attractive. But as we have already argued, there
are difficulties in holding that Essenes and Pharisees were related; in calendar, temple worship and interpretation of law there are as many differences
as similarities. The circumstances are better explained on the theory that the
new arrivals at Qumran were themselves Essenes. If the Pharisees incurred
Hyrcanus' wrath for opposing his High Priesthood, it is likely that the
Essenes, whose opposition was probably even more fundamental, were also
jeopardised by the quarrel which took place. If, as we have suggested, there
were Essenes living throughout the land at this time, Qumran would have

afforded an obvious choice of retreat, and their arrival would create little impact on the life and ideals of the community.

The difference between the community of periods Ia and Ib is not simply one of size, however. By the end of Ia the Teacher was almost certainly dead, and with his death would have disappeared that charisma and authority which had created the community. Adjustments were made in the expectations of its members; we find in a passage from the *Damascus Rule* a calculation that the End will dawn forty years after the death of the Teacher. Many of the features of Qumran life during period Ib become clearer when the departure of the Teacher of Righteousness is taken into account. Let us consider these under three headings: structure and organisation, daily rituals, and economic life.

Structure and organisation

To put it mildly, what the scrolls tell us about the organisation of the community is confusing. To begin with, we find legislation for the Qumran settlement and also for 'camps'. These camps have been taken to refer either to smaller groupings within the Qumran settlement – in which case the organisation at Qumran becomes nearly impossible to decipher – or to communities of Essenes outside Qumran. A third possibility is that the camps represent the organisation of Essenes at an earlier period of their history. In the last two instances, we should pay little attention to what is said about the camps if we want simply to know how the Qumran community was organised.

The first view is unlikely. It is improbable that at Qumran there would be two different orders of life, each with different structures and organisation. The *Community Rule*, which legislates for the Qumran community, stipulates smaller congregations of ten, but does not call them 'camps'; they are clearly part of the larger structure. Moreover, many of the laws governing the camps imply a community living within a non-Essene environment, including prohibitions against certain dealings with Gentiles. Such factors are more compatible with the second or third theories mentioned above.

As far as we are concerned, then, the 'camps' can be to a great extent left out of the picture, although in view of numerous points of contact with life at Qumran, the life of the camps may illuminate areas which the laws of Qumran leave dubious. We must also bear in mind, when using the evidence of Josephus or Philo about the Essenes, that it is possibly the camps which these authors are describing.

Let us in fact begin with the statement of Josephus that authority among the Essenes rested with the 'overseers'. The Hebrew word in the scrolls which corresponds to Josephus' Greek is *mebaqqer*. (The Greek word is, in fact, *episkopos*, also the title of the early church's officer which became 'bishop'.) The *mebaqqer* carried responsibility for instructing new members, and had final authority in matters of belief and practice. It seems, therefore, that he corresponded to the *maskil* of period Ia, although there may have been more than one *mebaqqer*, since a '*mebaqqer* over the work of the congregation' is mentioned. The title *maskil*, too, continues to be used, and a third name *paqid*, probably denotes the same office.

Josephus also mentions the Chief Priest as presiding over Essene meals. In the 'eschatological' (or 'theoretical') Qumran scrolls such as the *War Scroll*, the *Temple Scroll* and the *Messianic Rule* (or *Rule of the Congregation*) (1QSa), the Chief Priest is the supreme leader of Israel, at the head of the temple cult and, in 1QSa even superior to the Messiah of Israel. But what authority did the Chief Priest exert in the everyday affairs of the community? It is possible, of course, that he was also the *mebaqqer*. But a more attractive suggestion is that the Chief Priest and the *mebaqqer* jointly exercised a dual authority, perhaps corresponding to the ideal of post-exilic Judaism, of a messianic Chief Priest and a lay Messiah. This kind of leadership may be seen in the smaller groups, with a minimum of ten, to which the *Community Rule* refers. Each of these, it is laid down, must include a priest and one who 'studies the law continually regarding the right conduct of a man with his companion'. The latter figure may be the one elsewhere referred to as an 'interpreter of the law'. Of course, in neither case can we be sure that the second figure, the *mebaqqer* or the 'interpreter of the law', was a non-priestly individual. Indeed, most scholars would probably think otherwise. Perhaps we do better to confess that the confusion of offices in the Qumran texts is unlikely ever to be finally resolved.

We can observe some general trends in organisation, however; not only is the system more complex, it is also rather more democratic. Whereas in period Ia authority was vested in the *maskil* and the priests, we now discover a greater measure of authority vested in lay members. In a passage from the *Community Rule* which we take to be from period Ib, we read,

> They (i.e. the community) shall separate from the congregation of the men of falsehood and shall unite, with respect to the Law and possessions, under the authority of the sons of Zadok, the Priests who keep the Covenant, *and of the multitude of the men of the Community who hold fast to the Covenant*. Every decision concerning doctrine, property, and justice shall be determined by them (1QS 5,2–3; *D.S.S.E.* p. 78, my italics).

Whether or not the words in italics have been added to an earlier rule which originated in period Ia, (which seems quite likely), we have an extension of the legislative and theological authority beyond the priests to the laymen; indeed, to all the members of the community. Presumably, most decisions affecting the life of the community were now taken at a session or council of the community, which we shall describe presently, and whose existence we already know of in period Ia.

Some scholars believe that there existed at Qumran an inner council, consisting of fifteen men, twelve laymen and three priests. While this may be so, it is curious that we find only one unambiguous reference to this group, which is nowhere assigned any authority or any function. It is also possible, as others have suggested, that these fifteen men constituted the original nucleus of the community which established itself at Qumran. If this nucleus did once possess some authoritative status, this did not survive into period Ib. It is worth mentioning in passing that the various terms which the community used of itself occur in the scrolls in a way which defies logical synthesis or evolutionary reconstruction. 'Covenant', 'council', 'community' and 'congregation' – not to mention combinations of these terms – are in some cases obviously, and in most cases quite probably, synonymous.

The community during this period was structured in a rigid hierarchy, where every member had his own rank; this emerges clearly from the annual covenant ceremony, of which we shall say something in due course. There also appears, in the three 'theoretical' scrolls – the *War Scroll*, the *Temple Scroll* and the *Rule of the Congregation* – a system of military divisions into units of thousands hundreds, fifties and tens. This system is represented most fully in the *War Scroll*, where it becomes plain that the model is Numbers 1–10:10, describing the structure of the Israelites in the wilderness, prepared like a huge army for the invasion of the Promised Land. Surprisingly, many scholars have been content to include this system in their description of the organisation of the Qumran community, unaware of the obvious difficulties of applying it to a group of a few hundred. It is true that we find this structure in the description of the covenant ceremony in the *Community Rule*, on which occasion, it has been proposed, Essenes outside Qumran may have assembled at Qumran. But as presented in the *War Scroll*, where the organisation embraces the twelve tribes in a pan-Israelite context, the system quite probably belongs to Essene idealism rather than Essene practice. The fictitious list of treasures in the *Copper Scroll* should warn us of the danger of confusing real with ideal in the Qumran context.

The complexity of community organisation by this time is well brought out in the rules for admission of entrants. On this subject, the *Community Rule* confirms on the whole what Josephus says. The candidate first appeared

Plate 15 Looking west from the tower. In the background is the
aqueduct, whose point of entry into the settlement can be seen.
Here stand the remains of the large decantation reservoir and
the bath. Also visible is the beginning of the water channel
leading to the group of three cisterns in the western block, the
edge of one of them being on the left of the picture.

before the '*mebaqqer* at the head of the congregation', who considered both his 'understanding' and his 'deeds'. If these were found acceptable, the candidate was then admitted into the 'covenant' to learn all the rules of the community. At the end of this first period of probation the Council of the Congregation (probably the community in formal session) decided on his admission. A favourable decision led to his induction into the 'Council' (participation in sessions?), although he was not permitted to eat in communion with full members for a further year and until another examination. Nor, during this period, were his possessions reckoned with the communal property. After his understanding and observance of the Law had been tested, and on the authority of the priests and all the members, he entered the 'company' of the community, and his property was handed over. But still it was not contributed to the communal fund. The new member could now eat with the rest of the community, but not drink with them. This probably has to do with the doctrine that liquids were more easily contaminated by impurity than solids (as the rabbis also maintained). Finally, after yet another assessment by the congregation the new member was admitted fully, and was assigned a rank within the community. This rank was determined on the basis of his virtue in respect of 'Law, justice and the meal' – that is to say, his understanding of the Law as interpreted and obeyed by the community, his practical conduct towards fellow-members, and his observance of the requirements of purity. These three headings very well summarise the essence of life at Qumran.

All three of these, in fact, can be subsumed under the notion of holiness, the dominating theme of community life. Holiness involved not only scrupulous attention to the laws of Moses and the community's own regulations, but purity of thought and attitude. Concern to avoid contamination affected contact not only with outsiders but also with fellow-members. Josephus explains that a senior member (one of higher 'rank') would, if touched by a junior member, immediately bathe himself 'as if he had been in contact with a foreigner'. A similar if less rigorous attitude was adopted by strict Pharisees towards those Jews who did not observe the Law (including Pharisaic interpretations). In the same way we should understand the principle of communality of wealth at Qumran. Wealth could be contaminated by being mixed with the wealth of outsiders, or, as we have seen, of novitiates. It has been pointed out that this sharing of wealth has a parallel in early Christianity. According to John 13:19 Judas held the money-box for the disciples, and in Acts 2:44–45 we read that 'all who believed were together and had everything in common.' In the latter case, at least, the motives appear to be quite different from those of the Essenes, since the Christians sold their possessions and distributed their funds to the poor. There is no evidence that the Essenes did likewise. Furthermore, whereas one infringement of the Christian rule, recorded in Acts 5:1ff., was punished by death, the punishment at Qumran for such as offence was only exclusion from the communal meal for one year and the loss of a quarter of rations.

Yet punishments were not as a rule lenient at Qumran, and many of the offences referred to appear trivial. By this time, the rules of the community had developed further along the lines we suggested in period Ia; several more kinds of offences appear, including what we might call social misbehaviour. Disrespect to a superior, especially a priest, earned a year of penance and of exclusion from the communal meal; deceit, bearing malice, or slander met with six months' penance. Misbehaviour during community sessions was especially reprehensible, and sleeping during the proceedings was punished by thirty days' penance, two days' penance being exacted from any member who left the session more than three times without adequate excuse. Spitting during the assembly, or foolish laughter earned thirty days' penance. We may be fairly sure, therefore, that if these community meetings were sometimes boring, they were never light-hearted – or not supposed to be – and the very best behaviour was demanded. As it happens, the very existence of such laws shows what kinds of behaviour did occasionally occur, for one does not, as a rule, establish a regulation for an offence which has not been committed nor seems likely to be committed. On this line of reasoning, we could deduce that misbehaviour at Qumran was not uncommon.

In addition to the growing list of offences, we have a new kind of punishment, namely penance. It is a pity that we are nowhere given a clue as to what this entailed. It may well have meant extra duties.

Daily rituals

'Eat in common, pray in common, deliberate in common.' This is how the daily life of Qumran is summed up in the *Community Rule*. To this we should want to add 'work in common', but on this aspect of life the scrolls are silent. It is fortunate that we have Josephus to help us in this respect. He also tells us the daily rituals of the Essenes. They began the day by offering to the sun 'certain ancestral prayers, as if entreating him to rise'. The *Community Rule* puts it rather differently,

At the beginning of the dominion of light, and at its end . . .
At the beginning of the watches of darkness . . . and also at their end . . .
When the heavenly lights shine out from the dwelling place of Holiness . . .
And also when they return to the place of Glory . . . (1QS 10,1–3; *D.S.S.E.* p. 89).

The significance of these times for the Essenes was very great, for they mark the boundaries of the two domains of light and darkness, and their alternation in regular sequence was perceived by the Essenes as a symbol of the mystery of the order of things. A much-discussed doctrinal passage in the *Community Rule* sets out a belief in two equal and opposite domains, each created by God; each was ruled by an angelic 'Prince', the two representing Truth and Falsehood or Light and Darkness. The lives of all men were governed by these two opposing figures. As must by now be expected, this doctrine is not expressed with total clarity. Sometimes the opposing forces are clearly represented by angelic figures, but sometimes they are spoken of as influences struggling within the hearts of men. Sometimes mankind is divided simply into 'children of light' and 'children of darkness', sometimes – as in fragments of horoscopes found in cave 4 – each individual was understood to be made up of a certain number of parts of 'light' and of 'darkness', so that no clear-cut division between two kinds of men was possible.

After the morning act of blessing – Josephus continues – work was begun, each man being dismissed by the 'officers' to his own occupation. Work continued without a break until the fifth hour (late morning), when they assembled together in one place, changed from their working clothes into linen loincloths and bathed in cold water. Then they gathered in a special room, and went from there to the refectory which they entered 'as if they were entering a sacred shrine'. They were served, in order of seniority, with bread and a single course meal, the Chief Priest offering a blessing before and after the meal. Then, laying aside their garments 'as sacred vestments', they returned to work until evening, when they again dined in the same manner, eating for the most part in silence; if they did converse, those of lower rank always deferred to their seniors.

We cannot be sure, of course, how accurately Josephus' description applies to the Qumran community. But several clues suggest that his account is probably close to the truth. Although the scrolls say nothing about the midday meal nor about the work between meals, they do mention bathing and give us a description of the common meal. In both cases the information is a little indirect, but we have already seen that there is archaeological evidence to support the picture we have been given.

Let us consider first the bathing, which is a better term than 'baptism' because the latter carries misleading implications. The significance of Essene bathing has been very widely discussed, especially in view of possible connections with John the Baptist's activities and with early Christian baptism. We would probably be correct in saying, however, that Essene bathing did not have the significance borne in either of the other instances. It seems to

Plate 16 The bath at the north-west corner of the settlement, probably
used by members of the community when entering the
buildings after working outside. By comparison with the steps
leading into the cisterns, these here are wider and shallower.

have been primarily a rite of purity, and in this respect is closer to various
rites in Judaism. Bathing before meals was a necessary preparation for
eating, which seems to have had a sacred character. One conspicuous element
missing in Essene bathing is repentance; and we cannot be sure that there
was a special act of bathing or baptism which marked the entry of a new
member into the community. Yet the men of Qumran were in no doubt that
the physical purity endowed by bathing was quite inseparable from inward
purity. We can do no better than explain this in the words of the *Community
Rule*. An Essene who refuses to walk in the ways of God and rejects the
teaching of the community concerning the Law is unclean,

He shall neither be purified by atonement, nor cleansed by purifying waters, nor sanctified by seas and rivers nor washed clean with any ablution. Unclean, unclean shall he be . . . it is through the spirit of true counsel concerning the ways of man that all his sins shall be expiated . . . He shall be cleansed from all his sins by the spirit of holiness . . . and his iniquity shall be expiated by the spirit of uprightness and humility. And when his flesh is sprinkled with purifying water and sanctified by cleansing water, it shall be made clean by the humble submission of his soul to all the precepts of God (1QS 3,4–9; *D.S.S.E.* pp. 74–75).

The above passage gives us no reason to assume that there was any bathing at Qumran other than the regular ritual which preserved the bodily purity of the Essene. But where was this regular bathing performed? The Jordan river, the pool at Feshkha, and the cisterns at Qumran have all been suggested. There was, in fact, a bath near the north-west entrance to the settlement and possibly another in the south-east corner. There is no reason, then, to think that the cisterns would have been used for bathing, and the steps which were built into the side of them probably served to facilitate the drawing of water. There is also no evidence that the Jordan was used for bathing, despite the reference to 'seas and rivers' in the passage just quoted. On the other hand, it is unlikely that all community members were always able to return to the settlement at Qumran to bathe regularly, and so other bathing places must be reckoned with, especially at Feshkha. Josephus remarks, incidentally, that the Essenes regarded oil as a defilement and did not, contrary to Greek fashion, smear their bodies with it, but kept their skins dry. A probable reason for this was the difficulty of ensuring that the oil was ritually pure.

We now turn to the meal. Josephus gives the impression that all meals were of religious significance, and attended by all members of an Essene community. We must doubt whether this was the case at Qumran. The *Rule of the Congregation* describes a meal at which the Messiah of Israel will be present. The event takes place within the context of the future congregation of all Israel, but it has generally been understood that this eschatological banquet was anticipated in certain Qumran meals. This idea is well known to New Testament scholars who have suggested that the Last Supper may be understood partly at least in these terms, and perhaps also the parable of the rich man's supper in Luke 14:16–24, or the feeding of the five (four) thousand. There is a connection, certainly, with the Last Supper in that in this Essene meal bread and wine are explicitly mentioned. However, we cannot say that they bear any symbolic significance.

The curious deposits of animal bones, to which we referred earlier in connection with the question of sacrifices at Qumran, may point to certain meals at Qumran having enjoyed a special significance. If this was in fact the case, we can do no more than guess what occasions these might have celebrated. The annual covenant ceremony is one of the more attractive possibilities, but it is difficult to imagine that all meals at Qumran were compulsory rites of the whole community. Since some members of the community would have been working some distance from the settlement, it is most unlikely that they would have returned to Qumran twice or even once a day to eat. Nevertheless, the *Community Rule* ordains that any group of ten or more within the community should have in their midst a priest who would bless the firstfruits of bread and wine, which permits us to suggest that the regular meals of the community were celebrated in this way outside the settlement at Qumran.

After the evening meal, the *Community Rule* states, 'the congregation shall watch in community for a third of every night of the year, to read the Book and to study Law and to pray together' (6,7; *D.S.S.E.* p. 81). The phrase 'in community' surely means not that the entire community assembled together at the same place, but that this activity was understood as a corporate act and performed in groups – probably the groups of ten or more which have just been mentioned. What, then, did this activity comprise? The 'Book' in question probably means the Law, that is, the Pentateuch, the five books of Moses. It cannot refer to our Old Testament which had not by then received its canonical shape. The Essenes did, in fact, preserve copies of every book in the Old Testament except Esther, and to many of these, if not all, the term 'scripture' could be legitimately applied. Other books not in the Old Testament were also copied, so that we cannot reconstruct with any certainty what 'canon'   if any at all – might have been recognised at Qumran.

The importance of the Law at Qumran is reflected in the biblical manuscripts left by the Essenes. Of about 175 such manuscripts, 70 are of Pentateuchal books. The most important of them is Deuteronomy, of which 25 manuscripts exist. Deuteronomy has the form of an address by Moses to Israel just before entry into the Promised Land, in the course of which the Law given by God to Moses on Sinai is recapitulated. The great object of Essene reverence next to God, says Josephus, was the name of their Lawgiver, and anyone found guilty of blasphemy against it was punished by death. Outside of Qumran we know of this rule applied only to the name of God. In the *Temple Scroll*, where there is a re-working of the central, legal section of Deuteronomy, the words which in the biblical book are attributed to Moses are attributed to God himself.

It is also clear from the scrolls that the Essenes had their own interpretation

– amounting often to alteration – of the plain meaning of biblical laws, and 'study of Law' at Qumran meant not only gaining familiarity with the content of the Law but also understanding and interpreting its meaning according to Essene traditions.

At this point we may briefly digress to mention the treatment of the prophetic books among the Essenes, as revealed in the Qumran commentaries. The presupposition of these works is that the biblical text chosen for comment really refers to events and persons at the End-time, the period in which the community was living. Incidents in its own history were thus endowed with the greatest significance. The principle of exegesis is neatly summed up in the *Habakkuk Commentary*,

> God told Habakkuk to write down that which would happen to the final generation, but He did not make known to him when time would come to an end. And as for that which He said *That he who reads may read it speedily* (Habakkuk 2:2), interpreted this concerns the Teacher of Righteousness, to whom God made known all the mysteries of the words of His servants the Prophets (1QpHab 7,1–5; *D.S.S.E.* p. 239).

The technique of thus understanding present or recent events in the light of ancient prophetic statements is excellently illustrated from Matthew 2:15, where Hosea's reference to the Exodus, 'Out of Egypt have I called my son', is taken as a prediction of the return of Jesus and his parents from their Egyptian refuge. The view that the Old Testament prophets (including David, as the author of the Psalms) recorded what God dictated to them about the future without fully appreciating what they were revealing is still held by some people today. The Essenes and the New Testament writers were not at all unorthodox or unusual in holding this belief, but both differed in believing themselves to belong to a community within Israel within which the eschatological events predicted had begun to work themselves out.

Let us also consider prayer at Qumran. The scrolls contain hymns of thanksgiving (1QH), psalms, biblical and non-biblical (11QPs), blessings (1QSb, for example, which the *maskil* was to recite over the priests and the laymen) and several other liturgical fragments. Especially important is a work entitled the 'Song of the Sabbath Sacrifice' (4QShirShab), consisting of two fragments in which an angelic liturgy is presented, where the seven angelic princes bless the saints of heaven and earth. The editor of this text, Fr. Strugnell, believes that, having abandoned the tainted cult of the earthly temple at Jerusalem, the Essenes of Qumran believed themselves to be participating in the heavenly cult of the heavenly temple, a sanctuary which would in time be reflected by a true counterpart at Jerusalem. The idea of holiness which so permeated the community was reinforced, if not primarily

Plate 17   The base of the mill found in the southern part of the western
            block.

motivated, by the belief that life at Qumran was lived in the presence of
holy angels.

There is insufficient evidence in the liturgical texts to permit us to describe
the various acts of worship to which they may have belonged, but we must
suppose that the liturgy of Qumran was rich and worship an almost constant
occupation in one part of the community or another. A reader of these texts
will hardly fail to be struck by the overwhelming tone of gratitude, praise
and blessing which appears in such sharp contrast to the physical discomfort
of everyday life.

There is one important annual ceremony about which we are informed in
the scrolls, and to which we have already referred, namely the ceremony of
covenant renewal, which probably occurred at the feast of Weeks (or Pen-

tecost). Although this had originally been an agricultural festival in Judaism, and remained such for the Essenes, it had become, in the Judaism of the period, the occasion for commemorating the giving of the Law on Mount Sinai. The Essenes, of course, believed themselves to be the only true members of the covenant, and enacted a ceremony at which their covenant was renewed, and the status of each individual member was re-affirmed. It was at this time also that new members were apparently inducted into the community.

The ceremony, or part of it, is described in 1QS 1,16–2,25 and is modelled on the account in Deuteronomy 27, with the priests declaring God's goodness and the Levites confessing the wickedness of Israel. The entrants into the covenant then confessed their own sins and acknowledged God's mercy to them. The priests then blessed all the men of 'God's party' and the Levites cursed all the men of 'Satan's party'. After this, both priests and Levites joined in cursing all who entered the covenant deceitfully. This was apparently followed by the rededication of all existing members. Led by the priests and Levites, the members entered in order of rank 'so that every Israelite shall know his place in the community of God according to the everlasting design.' No man was to move up or down from his allotted place once it had been assigned, as it seems to have been at this ceremony.

Finally, let us consider the 'assembly' of the Qumran community. We do not know how regularly or how frequently this may have taken place. Perhaps it occurred daily before the evening meal, or, at the other extreme, when occasion demanded. Together with the meal, it was the focus of communal life. The *Community Rule* lays down the following rules for its procedure,

> Each man shall sit in his place: the Priests shall sit first, and the elders second, and all the rest of the people according to their rank. And thus they shall be questioned concerning the Law, and concerning any counsel or matter coming before the Congregation, each man bringing his knowledge to the Council of the Community.
>
> No man shall interrupt a companion before his speech has ended, nor speak before a man of higher rank; each man shall speak in his turn. And in an Assembly of the Congregation no man shall speak without the consent of the Congregation, nor indeed of the Guardian (= *mebaqqer*) of the Congregation. Should any man wish to speak to the Congregation, yet not be in a position to question the Council of the Community, let him rise to his feet and say: 'I have something to say to the Congregation.' If they command him to speak, he shall speak (1QS 6,8–13; *D.S.S.E.* p. 81).

Plate 18   A basalt millstone which had been thrown down a few yards
further south from the mill base.

Putting aside the difficulties created by the confusing terminology in this account, a problem we have met before, we can picture the assembly as a meeting of all members of the community, presided over by the priests and perhaps by the *mebaqqer* in particular. Subject to strict rules of protocol, every member present was given a chance to speak. But what exactly took place at these sessions? It is possible that the assembly was formally constituted whenever the whole community met altogether, whether to study the law, or to enforce discipline. The 'bringing of knowledge' to the Congregation could certainly refer to interpretation of scripture, since knowledge, something which the community prided itself on possessing as a token of its status as true Israel and as God's elect, included awareness of the real meaning of God's written revelation. But equally, this knowledge could manifest itself in everyday matters of legal interpretation, which were, of course, also based ultimately on the Law. Whether matters relating to the economic affairs of the community were decided by this assembly or in the hands of officers we simply cannot tell: as we have remarked, the scrolls are quite unhelpful in respect of the everyday work of the members.

Economic life

As Josephus has told us, the Essenes were scrupulous about the their cleanliness when participating in any religious activity, changing into special clothing for the purpose. By contrast, their working clothes are described as being very shabby,

> Their manner of dress and deportment is like that of youths being brought up in fear. They do not change their clothes or shoes till they are first completely in rags and tatters or worn-out with age.

Let us begin our account of the Qumran Essenes at work by surveying the duties which the routine of the settlement itself demanded. To begin with, is it likely that within the actual buildings the members would permit themselves to dress in such an unclean fashion? Since it seems that many unclean jobs were carried out within the buildings themselves it cannot have been possible to maintain them in a state of ritual cleanliness. There is a problem here which we simply cannot answer. But Josephus does tell us that because of the concern of the Essenes with purity, and therefore with the scrupulous preparation of their food, it was the priests who prepared the meals. There were, we know, kitchens to the north of the main block, but cooking may not have been always required. The diet at Qumran we know to have included bread, unfermented wine, meat (not necessarily on a regular basis) and dates. The bread was baked in a special oven close to the grinding mill, using flour from grain grown by the community, brought from the Buqei°a and stored in the western block. Meat was provided by the flocks and herds which the community could certainly have reared in the vicinity (probably centred on Feshkha), and date-palms grew on the plain between Feshkha and Qumran. We know that dates were eaten from the presence of date-stones among the ruins and in the caves. The only real problem which the Qumran diet raises is the wine. Was it possible for the community to cultivate its own vines? On this point there seems to be complete disagreement. Some experts have maintained that vines can be grown in the Buqei°a with considerable success. Others have expressed very strong doubts. Certainly no vines are presently cultivated in the immediate vicinity, but it is possible that the question will be resolved in due course by resourceful settlers.

The vessels for eating and cooking were all, it seems, manufactured in the settlement at the potter's workshop. (Also produced here, incidentally, were oil lamps. Whether the community possessed olive plantations – no doubt some distance from the settlement – we do not know.) While we are on the subject of activities connected with eating, let us recall that the washing of the refectory was probably a regular chore. No doubt the remainder of the buildings were also kept clean and tidy.

Some activities at Qumran involved building and maintenance. The aqueduct would require attention, with the clearing out of silt deposits and the replastering of cisterns and the channel when necessary. The store-rooms which were plastered would also require attention. Masons and carpenters must also have worked at Qumran. Although most of the stones in the buildings are rough-hewn, there are places, mostly at the entrances, where blocks are smooth-hewn. The mason's skill is best exhibited, however, in carved pillar-bases which were uncovered during the excavations. Where they had once stood, or were to have stood, we can only guess. They may have supported ceilings in large ground-floor rooms, or even formed a colonnade. The idea of a carved colonnade at Qumran may seem rather odd, but we might perhaps think of these pillar-bases as labours of love; even in a monastic settlement, where provisions were generally basic and the manner of life austere, the Essene mason could take pride in his skill and carve those things which in the world outside were recognised as among the most impressive and beautiful products of his craft.

The work of the carpenter has not, alas, survived as well as that of the mason. The beams which once supported roofs are now only ash. At some of the entrances to the settlement there may have once stood wooden gates or doors. In addition to these, it takes little effort to imagine the many everyday requirements which such a community would lay on a carpenter – tools, tent-poles, tables, and so on. The wood with which he worked was probably from the date-palms; even here, the community was self-reliant.

Other skills evidenced at Qumran are thatching and metalworking. Thatching requires little comment: the materials were again from date-palms, and perhaps the job did not in fact require special skills. There is a good deal of the metalworker's product remaining. An iron sickle and a hoe have been recovered, a scraper, perhaps, for cleaning out the pottery kilns, and a bronze cooking pot and inkwell. Nor must we forget the famous *Copper Scroll*. There were perhaps other crafts practised too at Qumran, mostly in the buildings of the western block. Here there would have been a lot of activity, with the arrival of provisions to be stored, and pack-animals requiring feeding. At a suitable distance from this busy area, the scribes were seated in the scriptorium on the first floor of the main block. Here the noise would be only the scratching of pens or the voice of the reader, if texts were being copied by this means.

We have already seen the long tables used in the scriptorium. If our understanding is correct, the scribes sat before these tables, a piece of leather or papyrus in front of them. Before commencing to write, the scribe drew lines across and down the surface to mark the columns, of which he could get three or four on to an average-sized skin. Using ink made from gum and carbon (another job for someone in the community!) he would write with care in a script which over the years developed in a way which enables any manuscript to be approximately dated (Plate 3). Palaeographical analysis of the scrolls is generally regarded as one of the most reliable of techniques whose conclusions provide an unshakeable foundation for dating the documents. But even so, a wide margin of error has to be permitted: we can trace the evolution of conventions of writing, but common sense will tell us that if the working life of a scribe can be as long as fifty years, during which his habits of writing will not necessarily change, and if elderly scribes sometimes taught young scribes, we should have to consider it likely that at any given time at Qumran a variety of styles of writing could have coexisted. It is a common error (especially in archaeology too) to confuse typological with chronological description.

As it happens, the majority of Qumran scrolls exhibit what is called the 'Herodian' script, typical of the late first century BC – middle first century AD. The handwriting may be either of a formal kind (such as one would normally find in official documents, etc.) or an informal or 'cursive' kind. The scribes copied sometimes from an exemplar and sometimes from dictation, or so it appears from the different kinds of mistake which each method can create. Where mistakes were made, the copyist often corrected

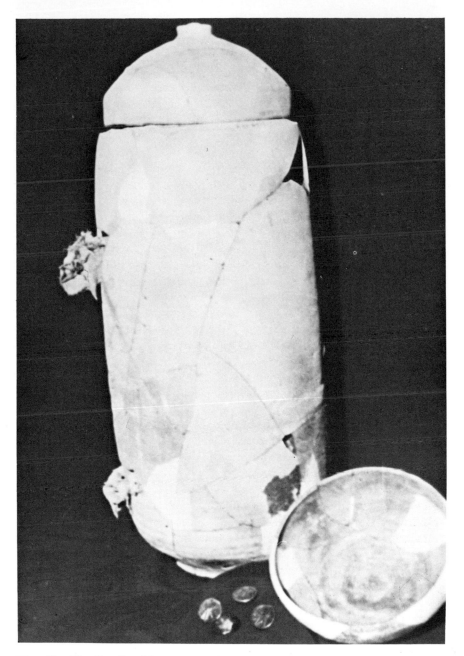

Plate 19   The Scrolls of Cave 1 were, it seems, mostly wrapped in linen and stored in sealed jars such as this one. Hence the generally good state of preservation of Cave 1 documents. Quite probably the contents were stored prior to departure from Qumran by the community which hoped to return later.

them himself. But in some cases the corrections are made in a different hand, probably by a supervisor or 'proof-reader' rather than a later reader or owner. So when the manuscript was completed, the scribe probably handed it over to be checked. The skins were stitched together, or the papyrus gummed and rolled up. The majority of surviving scrolls are made of leather, in fact, and the connected skins were bound round a piece of wood and the title of the work was inscribed on its surface. Such, at least, is the deduction of J. T. Milik, to whom has fallen the task of editing and publishing a large number of the texts. Milik adds that the scrolls were finally placed in a jar after having been wrapped in linen but so far as we know this was only in cases where they were meant to be preserved. It is unlikely that this was a regular manner of storage (Plate 24).

Most of the scrolls left to us are copies of biblical texts, and this is not surprising if study of the scriptures was one of the most important religious activities in which all members of the community took part. The familiarity of the Essenes with their scriptures is very evident in some of their own writings, which are full of biblical idioms and quotations. Many of these texts consist of biblical interpretation of one form or another.

One important question about the writing of texts at Qumran is raised by the recognition that the *Community Rule*, the *Damascus Rule*, the *War Scroll*, and possibly some others, are composite documents. Indeed, we often find fragments of already-known texts which contain significant differences from the document as previously known. All this tells us that the writing of some manuscripts involved more than simply copying; some of the literature was occasionally 'updated'. In what context was this process achieved? It is surely inconceivable that the scribes were permitted to undertake any substantial revision of a work which they were copying. If existing rules were amended or supplemented, the necessary revision of the documents was presumably made on the authority of the priests or the 'session'. But there was also scope for compiling existing documents or parts of documents into new works. The *War Scroll* offers a good example of this. Were there at Qumran men entrusted with the preservation, compilation and publication of Essene literature? If so, how closely was their work monitored? The answer to this question – if we could supply it – would determine for us how far we should regard the Qumran scrolls as 'official' products of the sect, bearing their own 'imprimatur'. Where there seem to be conflicting views in the literature, the explanation may be that within the community the scribal institution was not monolithic, but a variety of attitudes was able to come to expression in the literature. Was there even such a thing as private copying or editing or 'publishing' at Qumran?

From our own point of view, the work of the scribes is obviously one of

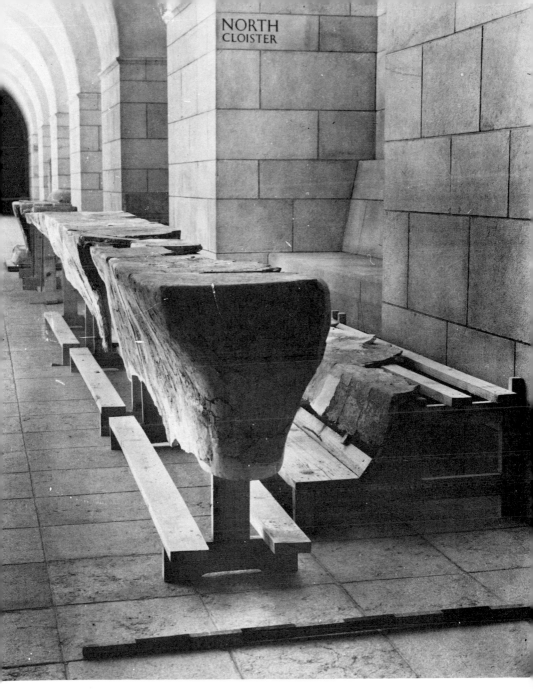

Plate 20 A reconstruction of writing tables and bench made at the
Palestine Archaeological (Rockefeller) Museum from debris
recovered at Qumran.

Plate 21 A view of the building at Feshkha looking north-west.

the most important, if not the most important activity to have been carried out at Qumran, and it was probably the privilege of very few members of the community. One of the objects found at Qumran was an ostracon, a piece of sherd, on which the letters of the alphabet were written in a crude imitation of a formal script. Perhaps this is how an aspiring scribe began his career. But let us not forget that the Qumran scribes were furnished with their raw materials by other members of the community. The ink was probably made at the settlement, and pens too, from the reeds in the Feshkha

region. The jars in which some of the scrolls were stored were made at Qumran, and so was the linen, although the flax must have come from outside. Also from outside came the papyrus, but the leather may well have been prepared at Feshkha, if de Vaux's identification of a 'tannery' is correct. As we saw earlier, this must remain an open question, and the installation in any case dates from Feshkha II (= Qumran II).

Feshkha is in fact more important than Qumran itself so far as the community's economy was concerned, for the buildings were apparently used solely in connection with agricultural and industrial activities. Feshkha has indeed been called the Qumran 'farm'. We have already mentioned, in addition to the tannery, the likelihood that community flocks and herds were watered here, and that the dates which grew naturally – and perhaps were also cultivated – were dried and stored. We should further bear in mind that until quite recently – at least well into the present century – the Feshkha area attracted many species of wildlife. In 1904, Masterman reported that Feshkah 'teems with bird life', and mentioned quails, partridges, wild ducks and pigeons. Conies and wild boars were also seen, and the pools contained fish. We cannot, of course, know whether the Essenes exploited this potential harvest, but they could easily have done so.

The reeds which still grow profusely around the springs and the pool are enormously valuable. The young shoots which spring up when the old ones have been cleared are excellent fodder for goats and cattle, and the large reeds themselves can be used – as they still are – for weaving such things as mats and baskets. The goats and cattle, of course, would provide milk, butter and cheese if these were part of the Essene diet as well as meat. Scope also exists here for the growing of some vegetable crops. Philo tells us that the Essenes kept bees, although there is no evidence of this at Qumran or Feshkha and, as we know, Philo does not apparently apply his remarks to Qumran.

A large quantity of bitumen was found piled on one of the floors at Feshkha, which prompts us to think of the Dead Sea also as a possible source of materials; salt, for instance, could have been extracted from it. Were such commodities utilised only for the community's consumption or was trade carried out? This is an important and interesting question. In an article which reviewed very optimistically the economic potential of the Qumran settlement[2] W. R. Farmer included the possibility that trade was carried out. In particular, the salt and bitumen from the Dead Sea could have been sold or exchanged for other goods. Bitumen, in fact, was once used for the preparation of medicines, a skill for which, Josephus tells us, the Essenes were renowned. The same may be true of potash which, Farmer observes, could be produced from burning the reeds, and would be used also for cleaning and as a fertiliser. One interesting suggestion was that even the scribes of Qumran might have copied manuscripts for use by Jews outside the community.

It is difficult to see how the question of trade can be answered with any degree of probability. It is obvious that the Qumran settlement was not completely self-sufficient; some needs had to be met from outside. The discovery of coin hoards at Qumran implies not only a community fund – of which we know from other sources – but also a use for coinage. The men of Qumran evidently bought what they needed. But we cannot be absolutely certain how far, if at all, they sold their own products. Wealth was acquired by the community by the acquisition of the funds of new members, which conceivably might have met its needs. We cannot rule out the possibility of interdependence between the Qumran Essenes and Essenes of other communities, whether in the form of trade or of direct financial support by these other communities, whose members perhaps earned their living in the society in which their community dwelt.

To return briefly to the Feshkha complex, we can conclude that a fairly large number of men worked here. In addition to the stores, workshops and enclosures, as well as the estate immediately outside its walls, there were first floor rooms which could have housed offices, or rooms for study, eating, perhaps even sleeping. It is not necessary to assume that those who worked here 'commuted' from the vicinity of Qumran. Two caves at Ras Feshkha were found to have been occupied during the period of the Essenes, although there is nothing to identify their occupants as members of the community. But although Feshkha affords us more scope for reconstructing the economic life of the community than the Qumran buildings, we are still left in the dark with respect to a number of basic questions.

Notes

1. For our purposes – and indeed for most purposes – the terms 'High Priest' and 'Chief Priest' may be taken as synonymous. The usage we have adopted here, while not consistent, is in accordance with the customary practice among present-day scholars.
2. W. R. Farmer, 'The Economic Basis of the Qumran Community', *Theologische Zeitschrift* 11 (1955), pp. 295–308.

7

Qumran prepared for War: Period II

The phrase we have chosen to characterise period II may be rather tendentious. It is certainly not possible to conclude that the ideology or way of life of the entire community was dominated by the prospect of war, at least during much of the period. But this feature seems to be worth singling out because it is one of the few respects in which we can distinguish the character of the community in period II from the preceding periods; and it is a feature which also reflects issues we know to have become increasingly dominant in Judaism as a whole during the first century AD.

Insofar as the organisation, ritual and economic life of the community is concerned, we have to assume that on the whole it remained as during the preceding period. The size of the settlement remained approximately the same and the buildings at Feshkha apparently continued to function as previously. However, between the end of period Ib and period II we have a gap in occupation (or at least large-scale occupation) of something like thirty years, or the span of a generation. We should hardly be surprised if some changes of attitude occurred during this time, changes, for instance, which would account for the resistance with which the Roman attack of AD 68 was apparently met. What we should dearly like to know, of course, is the story of those years of absence. Where did the men of Qumran spend all these years? Some scholars believe, as did de Vaux, that the community as a whole left for Damascus, because there are references in the *Damascus Rule* to a migration to the 'land of Damascus'; but such a migration is now thought unlikely. It remains a plausible view, however, that the Qumran Essenes continued their communal existence in the same manner as at Qumran, possibly in some other remote place of which we may never know. Alternatively, they may have dispersed to Essene settlements in different parts of the country.

Now, the absence of the Essenes from Qumran coincided very closely with the reign of Herod. While this may be no more than coincidence, we are permitted to speculate otherwise. There is evidence that Herod regarded favourably the Essenes as a whole. According to Josephus, a certain Essene named Manaemus (Menahem) greeted Herod, when the latter was still a boy, as 'king of the Jews', adding that Herod had been found worthy of this by God. He also slapped the future monarch on the backside as a token of the change of fortune which would finally beset a successful and glorious reign. When the first part of this prediction came to pass, Herod recalled the Essene in order to ask him further questions. He was unable to break Menahem's silence, but nevertheless 'from that time on he continued to hold all Essenes in honour'. On the basis of this account, some scholars have speculated that Herod came to value the support of the Essenes as he gradually alienated other sections of the Jewish population. Do we have any reason to believe, however, that the Essenes would be in any way disposed to favour Herod? The idea cannot be rejected out of hand, however unlikely it may at first sight appear. Towards foreign nations, and especially the Romans with whom Herod enjoyed good relations, the Essenes seem to have had at first an indifferent rather than a hostile attitude. In the *Habakkuk Commentary*, where the Romans are specifically referred to under the name of 'Kittim', their role is to punish the wicked rulers of Jerusalem. They are described as mighty and terrible, but do not incur direct condemnation. If these wicked rulers are the last of the Hasmonaean line, whom Herod replaced and whose line he finally exterminated, the Essenes may have felt no animosity to Herod or his allies. Herod paid scrupulous attention to the sensibilities of the most conservative Jews, made no pretensions to the office of High Priest, and accomplished a rebuilding of the temple; a venture which might conceivably have enjoyed Essene support, if Herod had offered the possibility that he might countenance Essene reforms.

Against this interesting theory, we have to set the contrary view. Herod, although a scrupulous Jew, was a patron of Hellenistic civilisation. He arrogated the privilege of appointing and dismissing High Priests, and according to Josephus the rebuilding of the temple was accomplished with the assent and under the supervision of the established priesthood. While there is no direct evidence to suggest that Herod persecuted the Essenes, such a possibility could account for the desertion of Qumran by the community, and their return as soon as the monarch was dead.

We have suggested that the attitude of the Qumran community towards foreign nations, and the Romans in particular, was indifferent. This attitude changed during this final phase of occupation. The opening decades of the first century AD witnessed outbursts of Jewish opposition to the direct Roman rule which followed the death of Archelaus, and this pattern persisted until the outbreak of war in AD 66. The attitude of the men of Qumran during this period can be followed in the columns of the *War Scroll*, a long and elaborate description of the Final War in which the hand of God would ultimately intervene to destroy the forces of wickedness. This strange doc-

Plates 22 Two copper rolls were found in Cave 3, but they were
and 23   impossible to unroll because of oxidisation. They were
          eventually sent to the Technical College in Manchester,
          England, where they were cut into strips in the manner shown.
          The Hebrew script can be seen plainly on one of the resulting strips.

Plate 24   The Psalms Scroll from Cave 11, a detail of which can be seen
on Plate 3.

ument has proved difficult to interpret, because so much of its description
is totally removed from reality, prompting the comment from one scholar
that it resembled an elaborate ballet. Y. Yadin, on the other hand, himself
a distinguished soldier, concluded that it was a practical manual for a war
which was expected to take place very shortly. Despite the many apparent
absurdities of the scroll, Yadin is probably nearer to the truth.

The *War Scroll* in fact unites two different tendencies within the eschatological expectations of Qumran, both of which we have already met. It has
both nationalistic and dualistic, pan-Israelite and sectarian dimensions. The
nationalistic, pan-Israelite war traditions which it contains outline an initial
campaign to reconquer the Promised Land and defeat the nations which
inhabit it. In the seventh year of the war, the first of the 'sabbatical' years
in which no fighting takes place, the temple cult is established along Essene
lines. The whole congregation of Israel is then mobilised for the remaining
years of a forty-year war in which all the nations of the earth are successively
defeated, and the 'dominion of Israel' established, '[sovereignty shall be to
the Lord] and everlasting dominion to Israel' (1QM 12,15; *D.S.S.E.* p.
140).

There is also in the *War Scroll* a description of a battle between the
'children of light' and the 'children of darkness'. (The Hebrew word can be

122

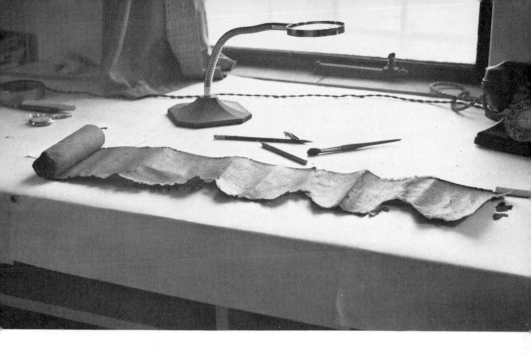

translated 'sons' or 'children' and both terminologies are used.) The battle consists of a single encounter with seven phases. In accordance with the dualistic doctrine found in the *Community Rule* (3,13–4,26), the forces of light and darkness are equal, and hence victory in each stage of the battle falls alternately to each side. In the seventh stage 'the great hand of God is raised in an everlasting blow against Satan and all the hosts of his kingdom' (1QM 18,1; *D.S.S.E.* p. 146) and the victory of the children of light is assured. The chief problem in this dualistic scheme is the identification of these children of light. The children of darkness are clearly defined as comprising essentially the Kittim, namely the Romans, although it is very likely that originally the forces of darkness were not identified. The emergence of the Roman army in this role can be shown to be an adjustment to political realities, which points to the first century AD as the probable time of composition of the *War Scroll* as we have it.

But who are the children of light whose victory over the might of Rome is anticipated? It is surely inconceivable that the men of Qumran, even in their most distant flights of fancy, could seriously oppose their own numbers to the resources of the mightiest empire the world had ever known. To begin to answer this question, we have to turn to the idea of the redactor who united the various conceptions of the Final War which already existed within the community, and produced a version of the encounter which reconciled the dualistic battle which effected the downfall of the power of darkness with the scheme of a forty years' war bringing Israel domination over all the nations of the earth. This redactor arranged his material in such a way that the great battle between the children of light and the children of darkness comprised the first phase of the forty years' war; now, instead of the initial six years being occupied with the defeat of the Gentile nations who occupied the Promised Land, they were devoted to a struggle between the children of light and the Romans, the 'Kittim'. In this, the redactor not only reconciled the conceptions of his different sources, but offered a more plausible account of the course of events, for any campaign leading to world domination would have to commence with the defeat of the Romans. Is this realism extended to the depiction of the children of light who achieve this initial victory? The redactor gives us the following clue,

> The sons of Levi, Judah and Benjamin, the exiles in the desert, shall battle against them in . . . all their bands when the exiled sons of light return from the Desert of the Peoples to camp in the Desert of Jerusalem (1QM 1,2–3; *D.S.S.E.* p. 124).

The 'exiles in the desert' are probably the Essenes of Qumran; but who are the 'exiled sons of light' who are to 'return from the Desert of the Peoples'? The expression 'Desert of the Peoples' is borrowed from Ezekiel 20:35. There it refers to a place to which God will bring his people from their Babylonian captivity, to renew the covenant with them prior to leading them again into the Promised Land. The context is therefore perfectly suited to the advent of the Final War. Nearly all commentators on this passage consider that the Desert of the Peoples is Qumran, but there are two objections to this conclusion. First, the phrase 'exiles in the desert' already refers to the Essenes at Qumran, and it is difficult to see how the following words 'when the exiled sons of light return from the Desert of the Peoples' can mean to refer also to the same group, unless the wording is extraordinarily clumsy. Second, the belief that the men of Qumran could expect to conduct unaided a successful battle against the Roman forces in Palestine is wildly unrealistic.

It seems more plausible, therefore, that the redactor is suggesting that his community will be reinforced for their confrontation by other 'sons of light' which can only mean other Essenes. These other Essenes could be either those living in camps throughout the land, or Essenes living in Babylonia, or both, depending on one's view of the sect's origins.

If our understanding of the *War Scroll* is correct, the Essenes of Qumran Period II became less isolated than during their previous history in two respects. Not only did they share in the nationalistic military aspirations of their fellow-Jews and join with them in their opposition to the Romans, but they also looked forward to the swelling of their ranks by other members of their brotherhood who lived beyond the confines of the settlement by the Dead Sea. As the ruins of Period II tell us, these aspirations died with those of the Jewish nation as a whole.

It is surely one of those quirks of historiography that we happen to know more about a fairly isolated and unorthodox Jewish community of a few hundred men than we do about the rest of Judaism during this very important period. The origins and early history of the Pharisees, the Sadducees and such institutions as the school and the synagogue remain obscure to us. This being the case, it is understandable that we should try to apply what we know from Qumran as far as we are able to the phenomenon of Jesus himself and of the early church. We must be warned, however, that the Dead Sea scrolls illustrate more than anything else the richness and variety of Jewish belief and practice in the time of Jesus. Moreover, as G. Vermes has recently reminded us, 'the enigma of the Dead Sea sect is by no means definitively solved' (D.S.S. p. 87). Widely-differing opinions about this community continue to be held; the possibility that we have miscalculated their origins and history remains a very real one. As to the beliefs, doctrines and hopes of these men, we may hope to be more confident. It is open to us to stand among the ruins of Qumran and, to adapt a phrase, 'think their thoughts after them'. These men may have been an enigma to their own age, and certainly will remain an enigma to a modern mentality which is so far removed from their own day. Yet to anyone who has stood and thought here by the shores of the Dead Sea, and who has in him a spark of sympathy and imagination, this settlement and its ancient inhabitants are more than a fascinating problem to the intellect; they are also a challenge to the spirit.

Indexes

General

Biblical References

Other Sources

Reference to other sources will be found on
pp. 69 and 81; references to passages from
the Dead Sea Scrolls are included among the
entries of the respective scrolls in the
General Index.